A DADGAD Christmas

By Doug Young

Cover photograph: Ed Claxton Malabar,
by Charles Webster

© 2013 Doug Young, Solana Press
All rights reserved
ISBN 978-0-9896349-0-8

w w w . d o u g y o u n g g u i t a r . c o m

DADGAD Tuning

All the arrangements in this book are in DADGAD - a popular alternate tuning for guitar. To tune to DADGAD from standard tuning, just:

- Lower your 6th string a whole step to D - it should sound an octave lower than the 4th string,
- Lower your 1st string a whole step to D - it should sound an octave higher than your fourth string, and
- Lower your 2nd string a whole step to A - it should sound an octave higher than your 5th string.

If you are new to DADGAD, the arrangements in this book should be a good introduction. Learning the tunes in Part I will introduce many common chord shapes and patterns and prepare you for more complex arrangements in Part II.

If you want to dive deeper into DADGAD, there are many resources for this popular tuning. My instructional book,

Understanding DADGAD For Fingerstyle Guitar (Mel Bay)

provides a comprehensive tour of DADGAD from getting started with one-finger chords to advanced concepts.

Acknowledgments

I'd like to thank all those who have taught and inspired me in my path in the world of fingerstyle guitar. Any book about DADGAD needs to acknowledge the contributions of the master of DADGAD, Pierre Bensusan, and of course, Davey Graham, who is credited as the tuning's inventor. Laurence Juber, Al Petteway, Martin Simpson and many others have also influenced my approach to DADGAD.

Special thanks to my wife Teri for her editing assistance, as well as Mike Nepper, Jim Jarrell, and Bob Evans for their feedback and willingness to spend time with Christmas music in July!

Table Of Contents

Introduction 4

About the Recordings 5

Part I: A Christmas Gig Book 7

All Through The Night 12

Away In A Manger 13

Hark The Herald Angels Sing.................14

It Came Upon a Midnight Clear 16

Jingle Bells 18

Joy To The World 20

Dona Nobis Pacem 22

I Saw Three Ships 24

We Wish You a Merry Christmas 25

Silent Night 26

Up On The Housetop 28

What Child Is This? 30

Part II: Performance Arrangements 33

Angels We Have Heard On High 34

Bring a Torch, Jeanette, Isabella 41

The First Noel 50

I Saw Three Ships 60

Joy To The World 70

O Holy Night 79

Silent Night 85

We Three Kings 92

O Little Town of Bethlehem 103

Introduction

A DADGAD Christmas is a collection of twenty-one arrangements of Christmas favorites for solo fingerstyle guitar, all in DADGAD tuning. The book is divided into two sections: *Gig Book* – a set of short, easy to play arrangements, and then *Performance Arrangements* – a collection of more complex performance-ready arrangements.

The first part of the book, the *Gig Book,* contains arrangements that are easy enough for beginner, but that are also meant to act as templates for your own arrangements. With a bit of practice you should be able to pull out these arrangements whenever you are asked to play a Christmas song and read the music, elaborating on the basic arrangements simply by adding your own variations within the basic structure. See page 8 for some tips on ways to enhance these arrangements.

The second half of the book, *Performance Arrangements*, features longer, more complete arrangements of nine tunes, ready to perform in any setting – with friends and family, in church, or in a concert.

These twenty-one arrangements also serve as a great introduction to DADGAD tuning, and hopefully they will give you some new ideas as well as some material to brighten the holidays.

About The Recordings

The companion CD to this book, also titled *A DADGAD Christmas*, contains contains recordings of both the *Gig Book* and performance arrangements. The *Gig Book* tunes are performed one time through in the simple form, as-written, and then a second time adding improvised elaborations. The elaborations aren't transcribed; they are intended to provide a few examples and some inspiration for developing your own enhancements.

You can download a digital version – in a variety of formats – of the companion CD completely free from http://store.dougyoungguitar.com or you can purchase a jewel-case CD from Amazon. The CD can also be purchased from itunes or CD Baby.

CD Tracks

1. The First Noel
2. Angels We Have Heard on High
3. I Saw Three Ships
4. Away In a Manger
5. Dona Nobis Pacem
6. Joy to the World
7. Hark the Herald Angels Sing
8. Up on the Housetop
9. Silent Night
10. It Came Upon a Midnight Clear
11. What Child is This?
12. O Holy Night
13. We Three Kings
14. All Through the Night
15. Bring a Torch, Jeanette, Isabella
16. Jingle Bells
17. I Saw Three Ships (GB)
18. Joy to the World (GB)
19. Silent Night (GB)
20. We Wish You a Merry Christmas
21. O Little Town of Bethlehem

About The Author

Doug Young is a fingerstyle guitarist, composer and arranger from the San Francisco Bay Area. He is a Contributing Editor for Acoustic Guitar magazine, and the author of the best selling Mel Bay instructional book *Understanding DADGAD for Fingerstyle Guitar,* as well as *Acoustic Guitar Amplification Essentials* by String Letter Publishing. Doug has released two CDs, *Laurel Mill* (2003) and *Closing Time* (2011). His composition "Autumn Roads" from *Closing Time* won Best Instrumental (2011) from the International Acoustic Music Awards (IAMA).

Part I – A Christmas Gig Book

Christmas and acoustic guitar make a great combination, and as guitarists, we are more likely to find an appreciative audience for the harp-like tones of solo fingerstyle guitar during the holidays than any other time. But since Christmas only comes around once a year, you may not have a set of tunes prepared and ready to go when you get a request to play for a gathering, friends or family.

My solution to the challenge is this *Gig Book*, a collection of popular Christmas tunes designed to be simple enough to basically sight read – or at least be able to learn easily and play while referring to the tab. You can think of this collection of tunes as a "fake book" for fingerstyle players - templates around which to create your own arrangements. These are arrangements that you can play with little or no practice, with the music in front of you. Each arrangement is full enough to stand on its own as written, but also simple enough to serve as an outline that you can embellish in the moment. All the tunes are designed to fit on either a single page or facing pages so you won't need to turn pages. And of course, since all the arrangements are in DADGAD, you won't need to disrupt your performance by retuning between songs.

Gig Book Tips

The goal of the *Gig Book* is to provide a collection of the simplest arrangements possible so that you can not only perform each tune while reading the music, but also embellish the arrangement according to your own tastes. Most of the *Gig Book* arrangements consist of a single pass, or in some cases, a few passes through each tune. One way to extend an arrangement is simply to repeat it as many times as you like. Repeating the tune exactly as written is likely to get a bit boring unless you're just providing background music, so you will probably want to create some variations on each additional pass. These variations don't need to be elaborate or complicated; in fact, you can create a lot of variety and interest simply by changing dynamics, phrasing and tone, even if you leave the notes exactly as written.

However, the goal of these arrangements is to be simple enough that you can easily change them, even on the fly, to add your own variations. Let's look at one example. Here's the first phrase of *Away in a Manger*, as written:

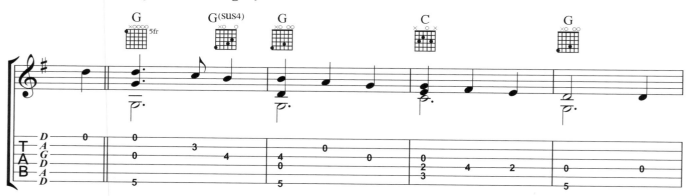

The second time you play the tune, you might add a few extra bass notes or other notes within the chords, and perhaps vary the timing a little. In most of these arrangements, the melody and accompaniment are based around chord shapes, so it should be fairly easy to introduce additional bass notes from within the chord. For example, consider the following variation:

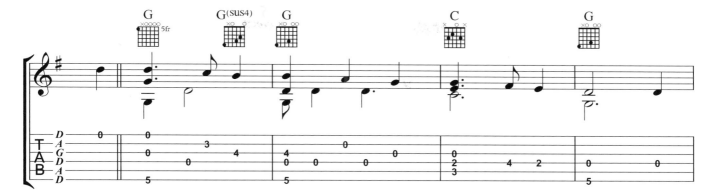

The third time through, you might add more arpeggios – just pick various notes within the chord shape. If you are careful to continue to bring out the melody, you can create a complex-sounding piece with inner moving voices just by adding patterns over the chord shapes. For example:

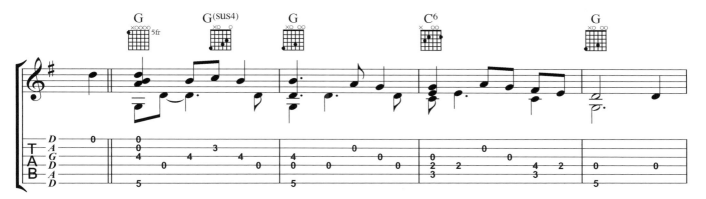

Once you are comfortable with a tune, you may find more extensive ways to enhance the basic arrangement. Here's an example that takes more liberties. You can still think of measures 3 and 4 as being based on the original chord shapes – but this version introduces a bass line that moves down against the melody.

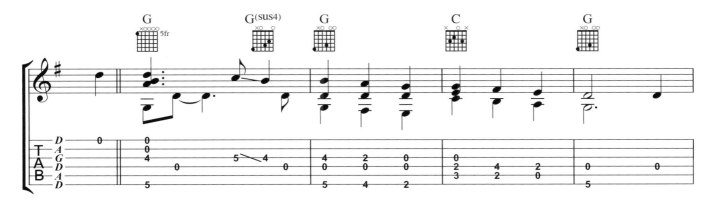

Gig Book Performance Notes

All Through The Night

I arranged this Welsh melody in the key of C – an often overlooked choice in DADGAD – and provides a good exercise in the I-IV-ii-V progression. The arrangement is based strongly around the chord shapes as shown, so it is straightforward to add arpeggios to fill out the sound.

Away In A Manger

This arrangement is in the key of G, which is one of the richest-sounding keys in DADGAD. The opening line is a descending G-major scale, so I'm exploiting one of DADGAD's most useful features – the cross-string harp effect created by playing consecutive notes of a scale on different strings.

Hark The Herald Angels Sing

The repetitious melody notes in this tune lend themselves to some moving bass lines and inner voices. For example, the opening measure moves from a D to a D/F#, while measure 3 uses a moving harmony line against the melody to add some interest. The high melody starting at measure 13 may take some practice. Remember that the melody is the most important thing, so if you have trouble grabbing the chord shapes, it's fine to drop the inner voices or even the bass notes.

It Came Upon a Midnight Clear

Here's another arrangement in the key of C, which lets us take advantage of some rich chord voicings for F and G. The biggest challenge is probably measures 18 and 19. E is a somewhat difficult chord in DADGAD, so be careful about hitting open strings that don't fit the chord.

Jingle Bells

This arrangement uses an alternating bass. I'm fingering the G chord to allow the bass notes to fall on the 5th and 6th strings. You could alternate between the 4th and 6th, but using the 5th string makes it a littler easier to mute the strings with your palm, which creates a distinctive tight bass sound. This technique also makes the open D on the 4th string stand out better when it is used in the melody, such as in measure 10.

Joy To The World

Joy to the World is mostly an exercise in playing harmonized 6ths, over an alternating bass line. Because this arrangement is less chord-based, it is somewhat more difficult to take liberties with the arrangement, but you can still vary time, dynamics, tone, tempo, and more, to create some interest on additional verses.

Dona Nobis Pacem

This beautiful chant is challenging to arrange because the basic melody is so short. Here, I've developed the tune a bit with multiple verses, starting with a single-line unaccompanied melody, and adding more parts with each pass. You could apply this approach to any of these arrangements, playing the melody one time through with no accompaniment. The cross-string sections provide an opportunity to leverage DADGAD to create a sustaining harp-like effect.

I Saw Three Ships

This is another example of a *very* short tune. The melody is only 8 bars long, and consists of two nearly-identical 4-bar sequences, with only two chords for harmony. I've written it out in two octaves, and you can alternate between them, varying the timing and phrasing. You can extend a tune like this by improvising alternate sections, even something as simple as just playing the chords by themselves. See the full performance version on page 60 for some other ideas.

We Wish You a Merry Christmas

This happy tune dates from 16th century England. Be careful of the E chord in measure 6. Otherwise, this should be an easy tune to play.

Silent Night

This arrangement contains two separate versions, one in the key of D, and another in the key of A. The last chord of each section sets up a modulation to the next key. You could choose to stay in just one key or the other, repeat each key several times before modulating, or repeat the entire arrangement as written, modulating back and forth. You can end the tune in either key by stopping before the 7th chord that sets up the next key change.

Up On The Housetop

This is another example of an arrangement in two keys, with a modulation between them. In this case, I placed the tune in the keys of D and G. I'm using an alternating bass line, so try to play with a palm mute on the lower strings.

What Child Is This?

Because it is based on the classic renaissance tune, *Greensleeves*, this tune can be played year round. The tune is in A minor. Watch the fingerings, especially the transitions around the E chord. Measure 27 uses harmonized thirds to provide some contrast, but you could also play this measure the same as measure 19 and maintain the bass notes.

All Through The Night

DADGAD Tuning

Welsh folk song (circa 1784), arr by Doug Young

Away in a Manger

DADGAD Tuning

Traditional, arr by Doug Young

Hark, The Herald Angels Sing

DADGAD Tuning

Wesley (circa 1739), arr by Doug Young

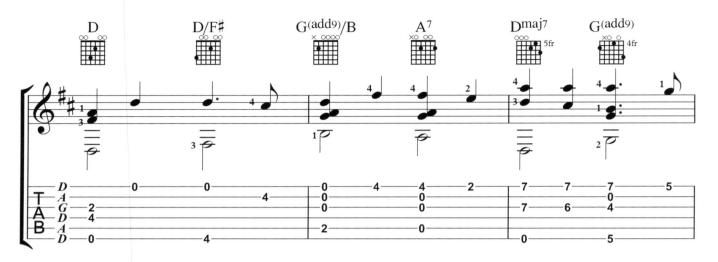

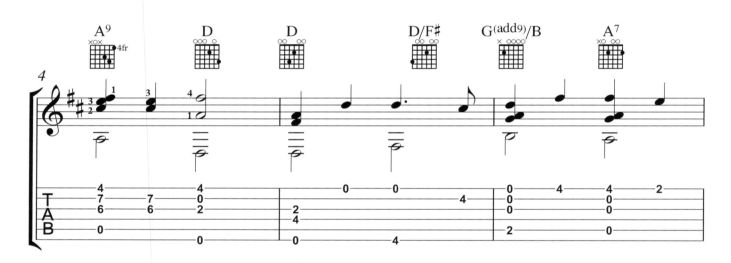

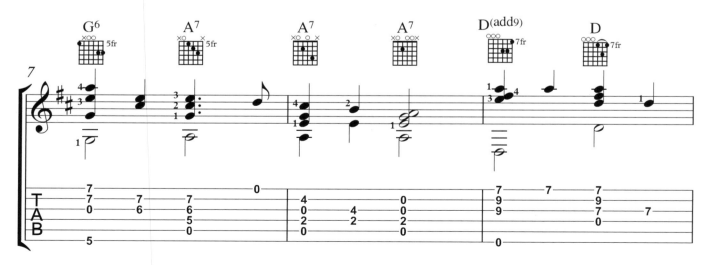

Hark, The Herald Angels Sing

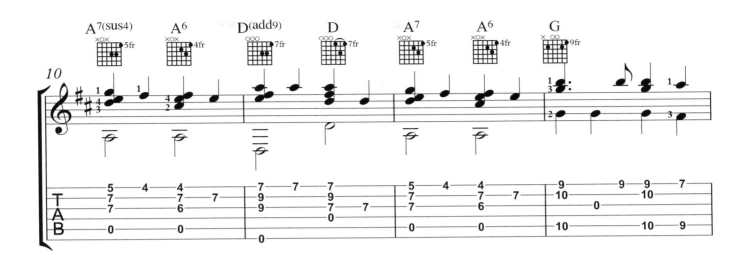

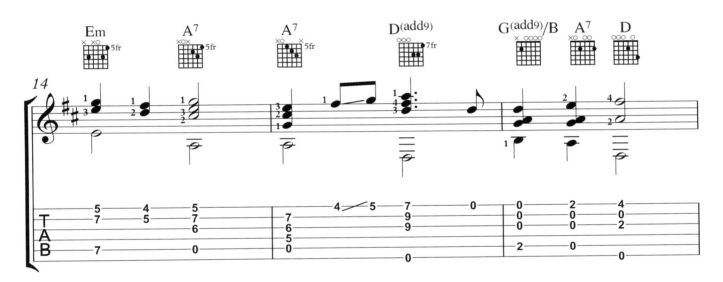

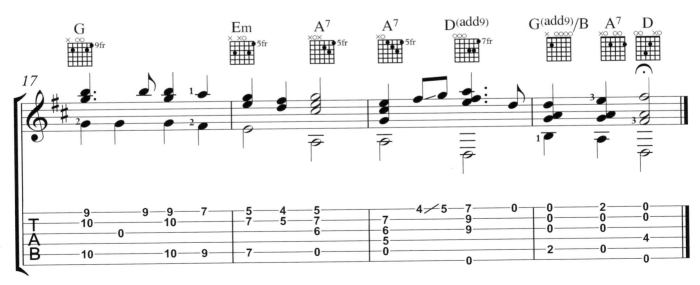

It Came Upon a Midnight Clear

DADGAD Tuning

Sears/Willis (circa 1849), arr Doug Young

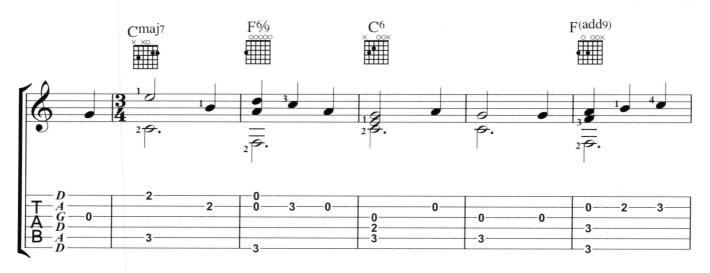

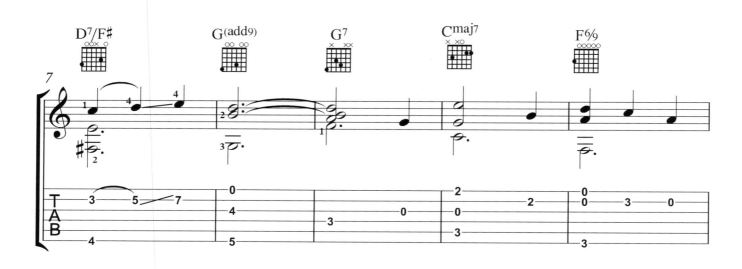

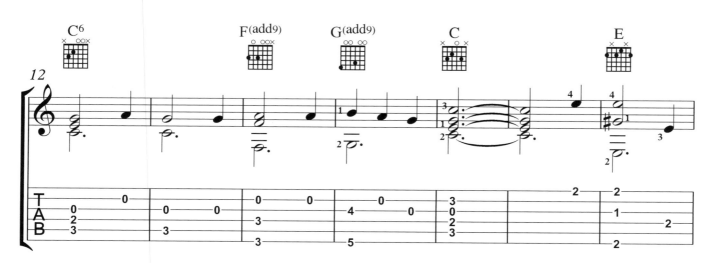

It Came Upon a Midnight Clear

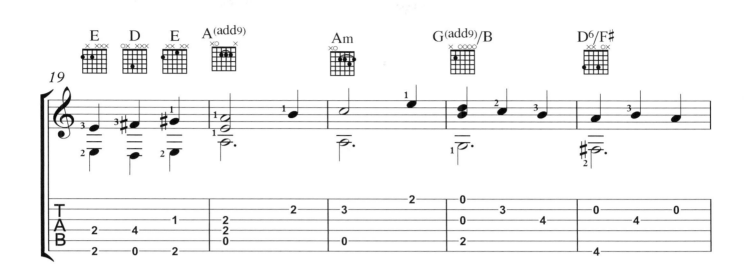

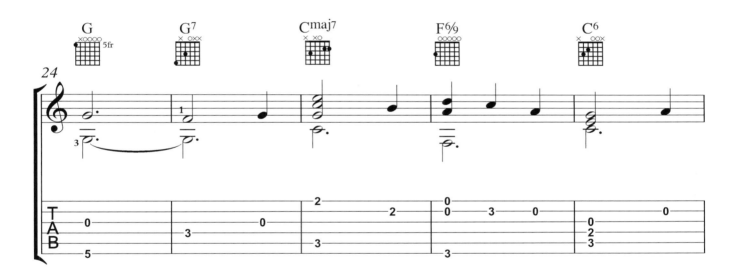

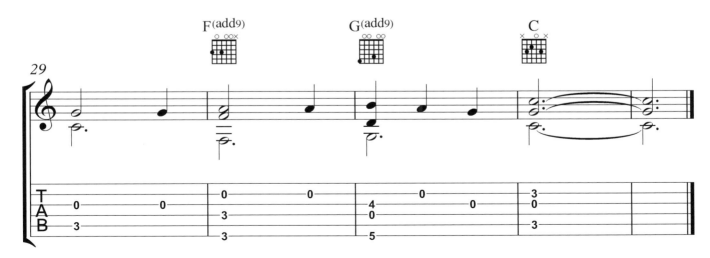

Jingle Bells

DADGAD Tuning

Pierpont (curca 1857), arr Doug Young

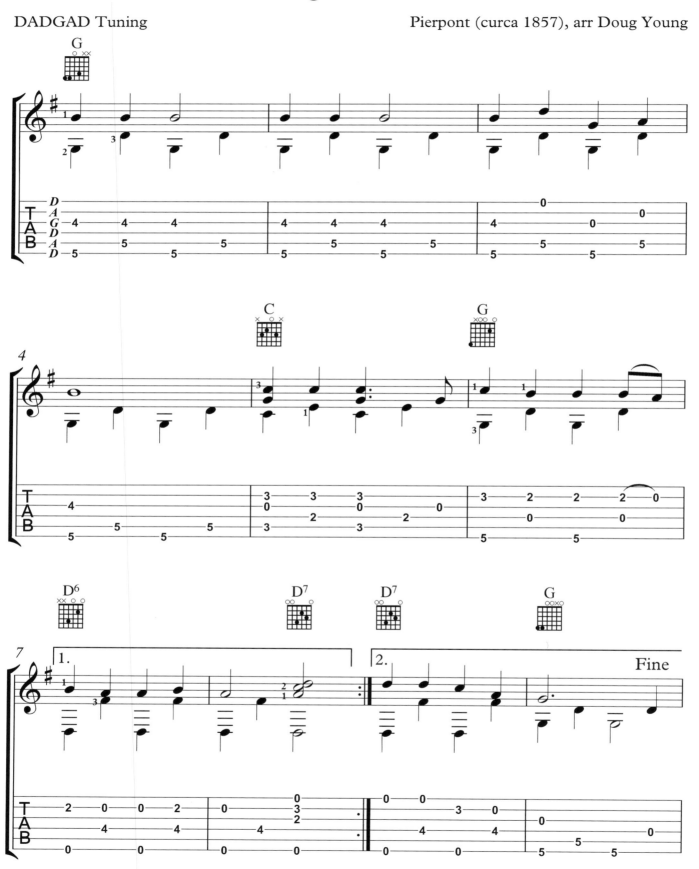

Jingle Bells

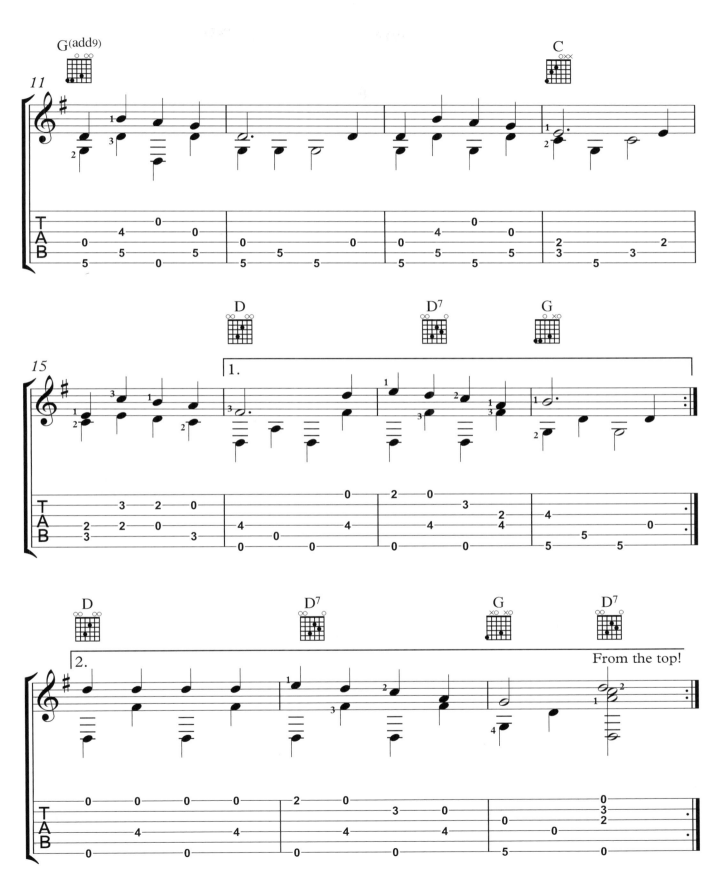

Joy To The World

DADGAD Tuning

Watts/Mason (circa 1719), arr by Doug Young

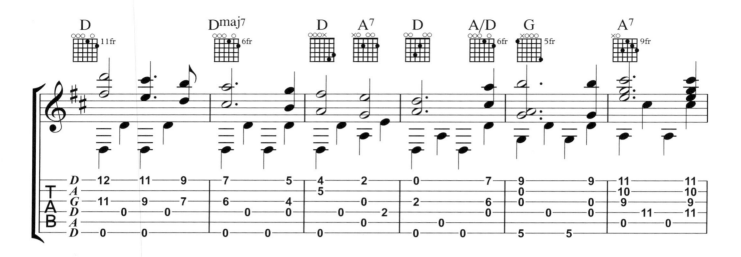

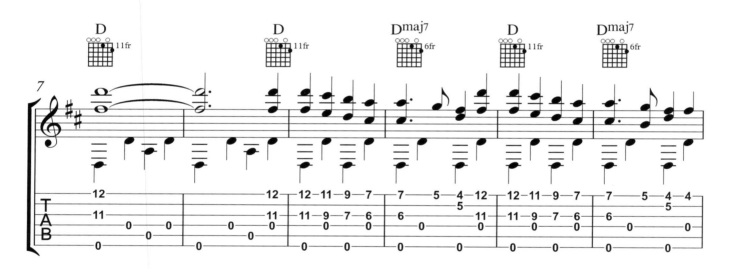

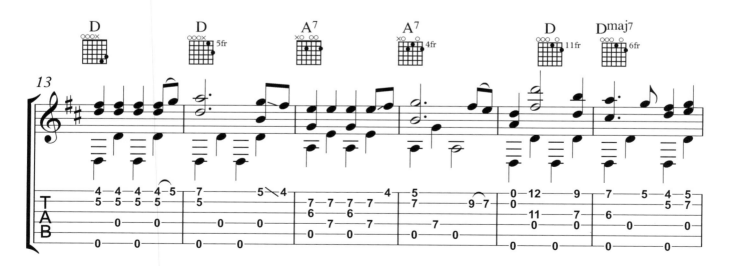

Joy To The World

Dona Nobis Pacem

DADGAD Tuning

Traditional, arr Doug Young

Dona Nobis Pacem

I Saw Three Ships

DADGAD Tuning

Traditional (17th century), arr Doug Young

We Wish You a Merry Christmas

DADGAD Tuning

Tradditional (16th century), arr Doug Young

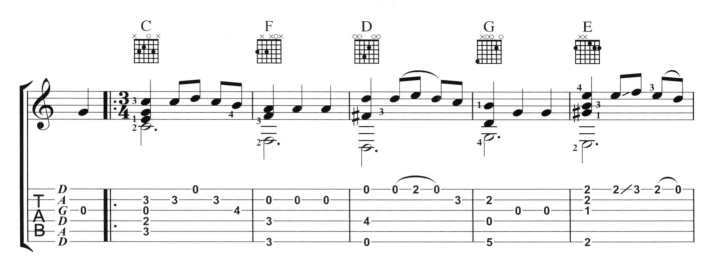

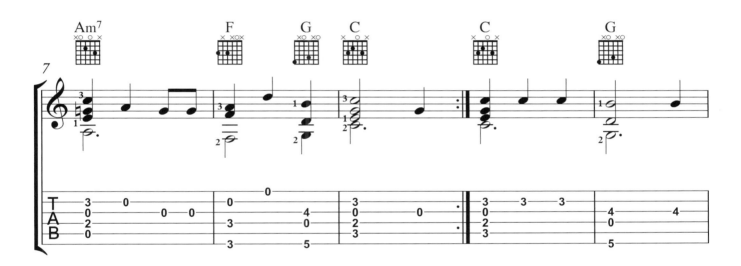

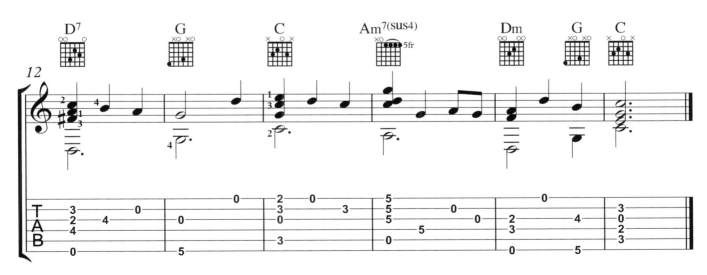

Silent Night

DADGAD Tuning

Mohr/Gruber (circa 1818), arr Doug Young

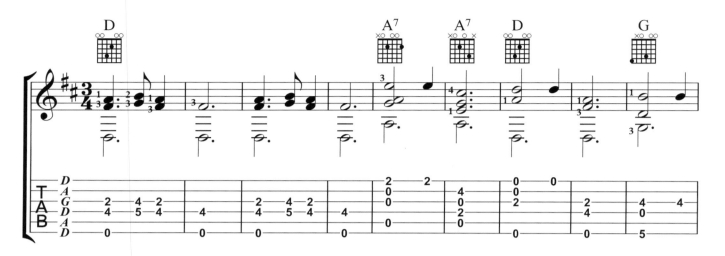

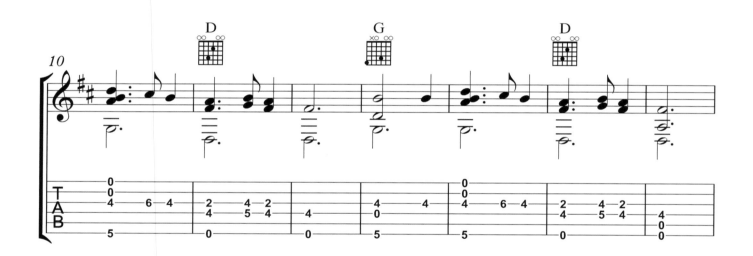

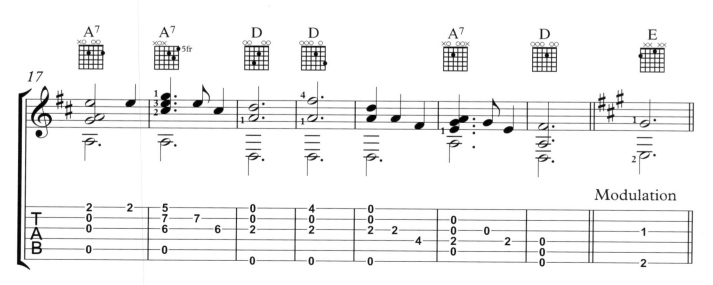

Modulation

Silent Night

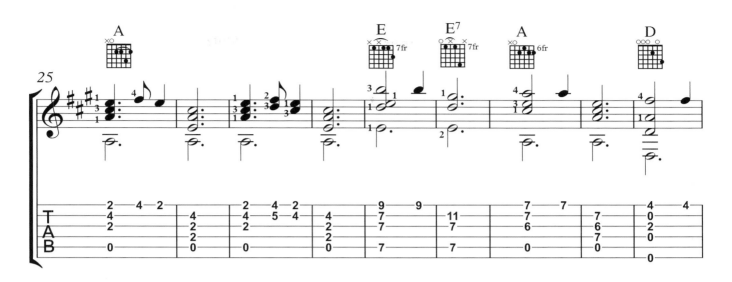

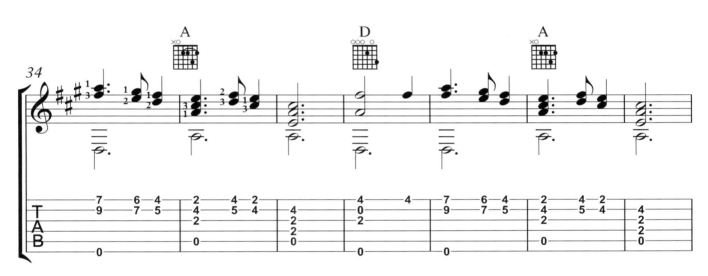

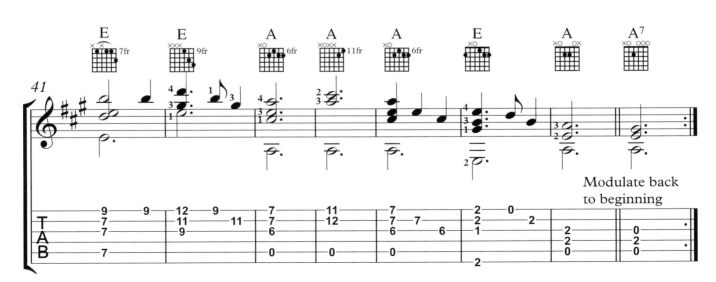

Modulate back
to beginning

Up On The Housetop

DADGAD Tuning

Hanby (circa 1864), arr Doug Young

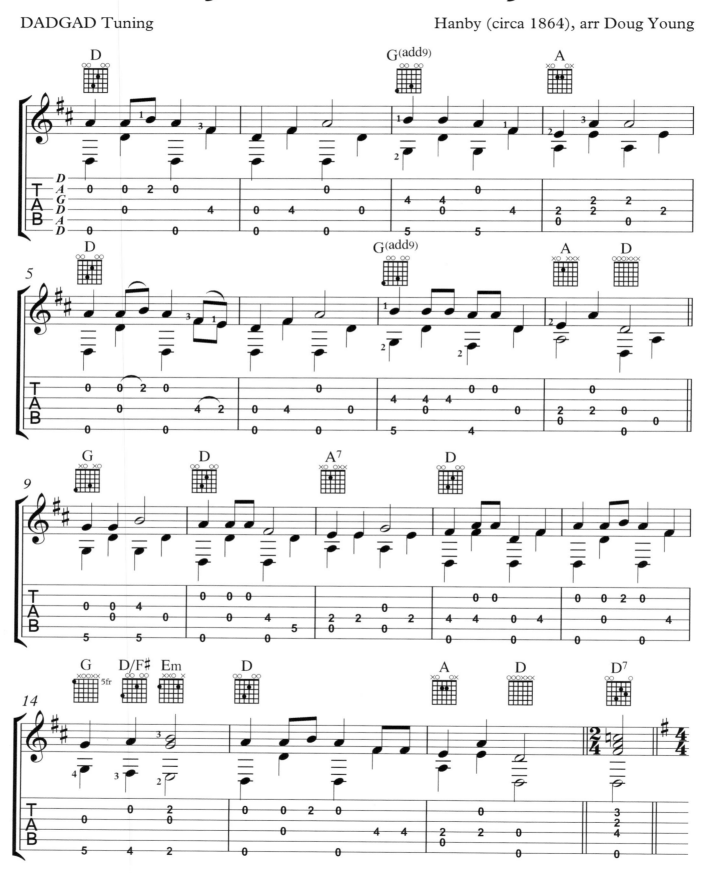

Up On The Housetop

What Child Is This?

DADGAD Tuning

Dix (circa 1865), arr Doug Young

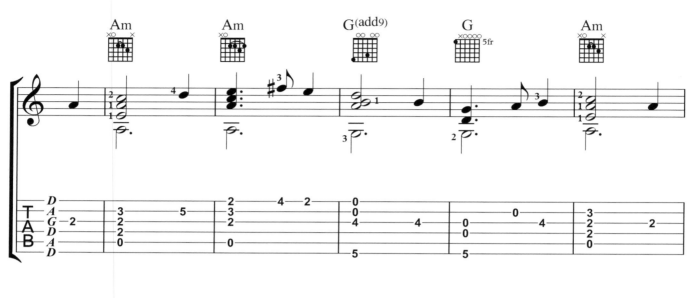

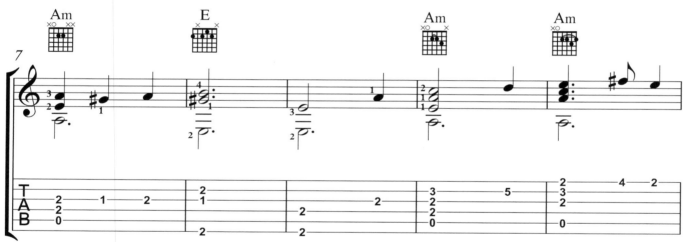

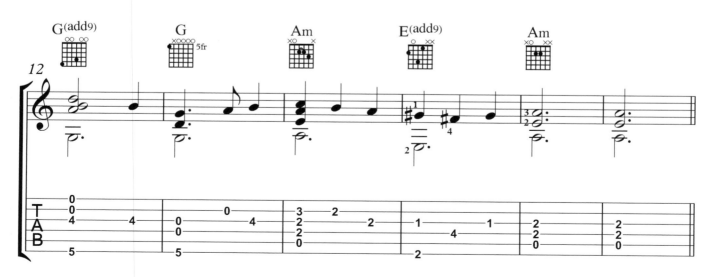

What Child Is This?

Part II – Performance Arrangements

The arrangements in this section should be suitable for any occasion from playing for family in front of the fireplace to concert-level performances. Unlike the short and basic *Gig Book* arrangements, these tunes are developed to a performance length, explore melodic and harmonic variations, and also add introductions and other extended thematic elements. The pieces aren't necessarily difficult, and should be accessible to an intermediate guitarist, although they are more challenging than the Gig Book arrangements. Perhaps the biggest change from the simpler Gig Book tunes is that in these arrangements I felt free to do whatever I thought would sound good, without worrying about sticking within basic chord shapes or making it simple to create variations, and of course the arrangements extend well beyond one or two pages.

You'll notice that there are a few tunes in this section that also appear in the simpler arrangements in the the Gig Book section. Some carols are worth multiple arrangements! You might also find some ideas that you can take back and incorporate into the simpler versions.

I hope you enjoy learning and playing any of these that strike your fancy!

Angels We Have Heard On High

Angels We Have Heard on High is an 18th century carol whose words celebrate the appearance of angels at the time of Jesus' birth. The words to the song are based on a traditional French carol, *Les Dans Nos Campagnes*. Like many Christmas hymns, the lyrics are sometimes sung over several different melodies. The melody arranged here is the one most commonly used for the song – another traditional hymn, *Gloria*.

Besides being a staple among carolers and churches at Christmas time, *Angels We Have Heard on High* has been recorded by everyone from the Carpenters to REO Speedwagon.

This arrangement is in the key of G, a great key in DADGAD because of the beautiful Gadd9 chord. I've also leveraged some other rich-sounding chords – Cmaj7, Em9 and more – to enhance the tune.

The chorus is the most memorable part of the tune, and when sung, the sustained melismatic notes provide a sharp contrast to the verse. Melodies that rely on sustain present a special challenge in solo guitar arrangements. In this case, I've tried to place the main melody notes on open strings, and create a sense of motion with harp-like arpeggios under the melody. Try to let the melody notes ring out and avoid cutting them off as you change chords.

Try to hold the G bass note down throughout the intro riff, but you can probably get away with lifting your finger if the stretch is too much. The second verse, in the higher octave also requires some serious stretches to include the bass notes. There are some alternatives, including dropping bass notes, as well as taking them up an octave, but you should be able to make these reaches with practice!

Angels We Have Heard On High

DADGAD Tuning

Traditional, arr by Doug Young

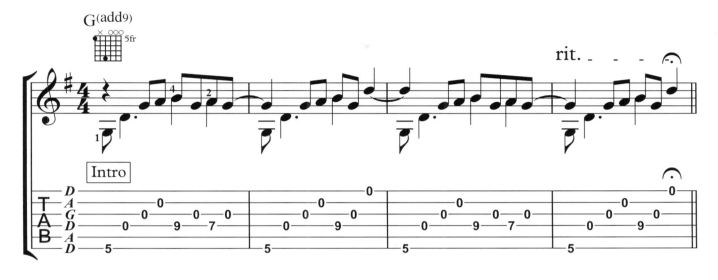

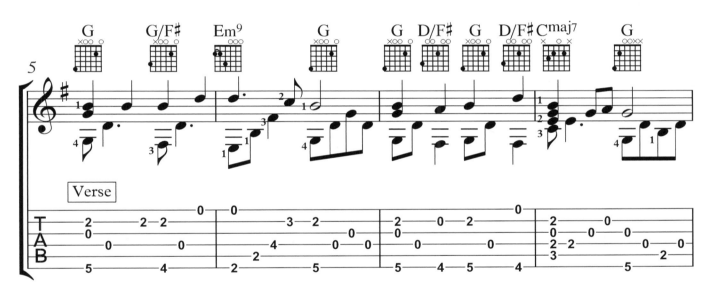

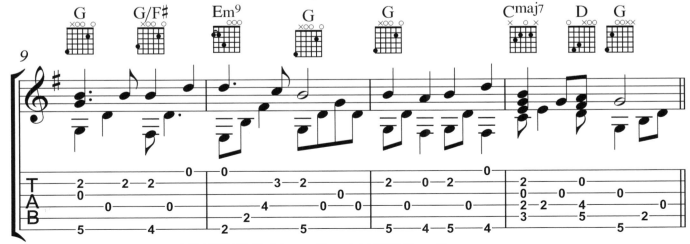

Angels We Have Heard On High

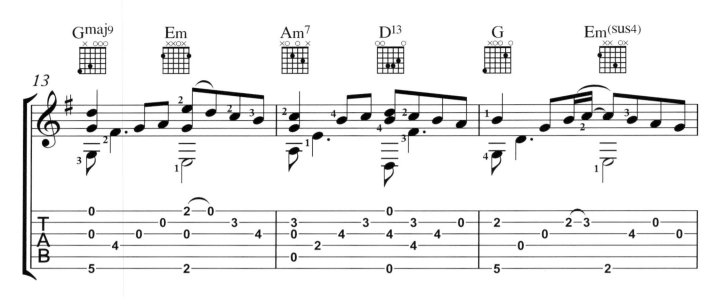

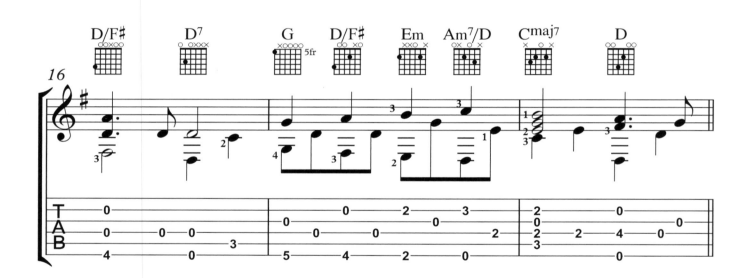

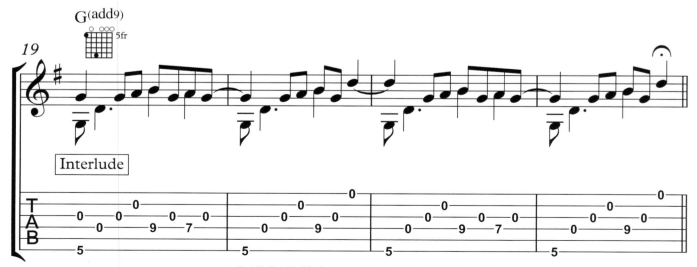

Angels We Have Heard On High

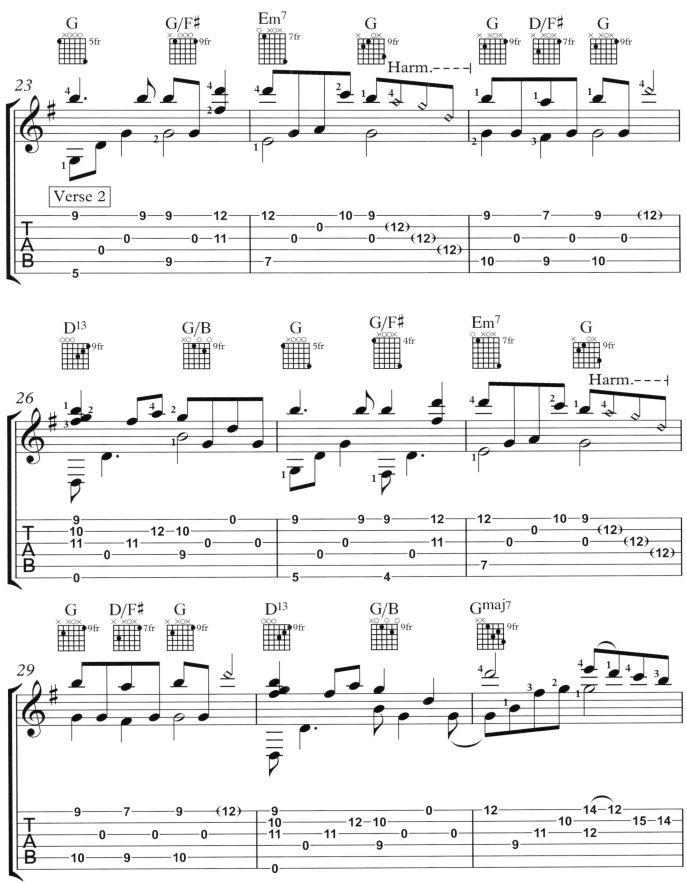

Angels We Have Heard On High

Angels We Have Heard On High

Angels We Have Heard On High

Bring a Torch, Jeannette, Isabella

Bring a Torch, Jeanette, Isabella is a 16th century song from the Provence region of France. The melody is based on an even older air.

My arrangement of *Bring a Torch* began in DGDGAD, a close relative to DADGAD. DADGAD works well in the key of G, and lowering the 5th string down to G makes it even easier to play the tonic of the key without fretting. However, here I've reworked the arrangement for DADGAD, and it still works well. The introduction is based on a rhythmic 12th fret harmonic pattern, and then transitions to a fanfare section that hints at the tune to come. Shortened forms and variations on the introduction are also used as interludes between verses.

The verse introduces variations, some of which are fairly subtle. In performing this tune, I tend to mix and match these different ideas as the mood strikes. The third verse, starting at measure 103, differs most from the others. I start by drop the bassing, and also use a hammer-on-from-nowhere technique to produce some contrast to the other verses.

Bring a Torch, Jeannette, Isabella

DADGAD Tuning

Traditional, arr Doug Young

Bring a Torch, Jeanette, Isabella

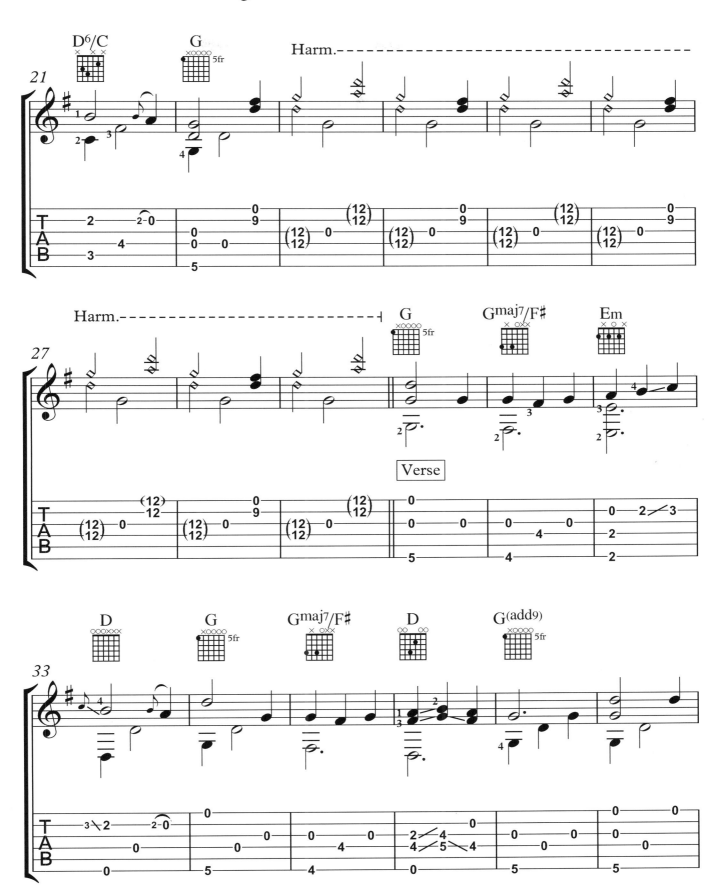

Bring a Torch, Jeanette, Isabella

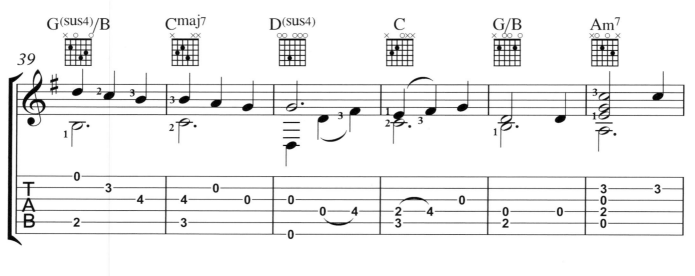

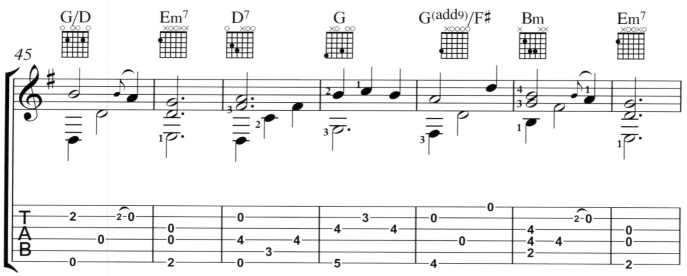

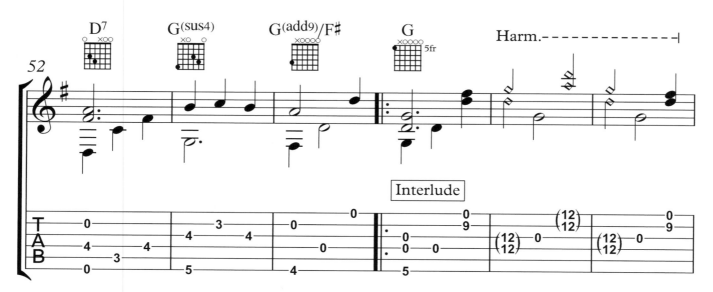

Bring a Torch, Jeanette, Isabella

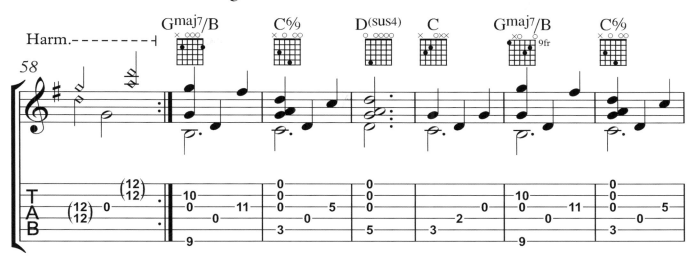

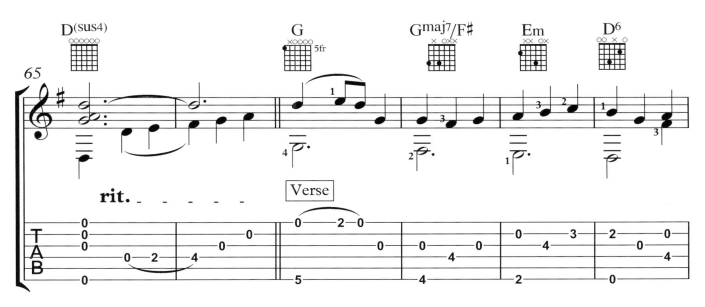

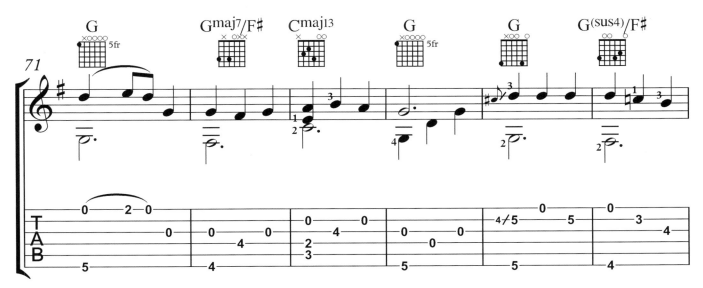

Bring a Torch, Jeanette, Isabella

Bring a Torch, Jeanette, Isabella

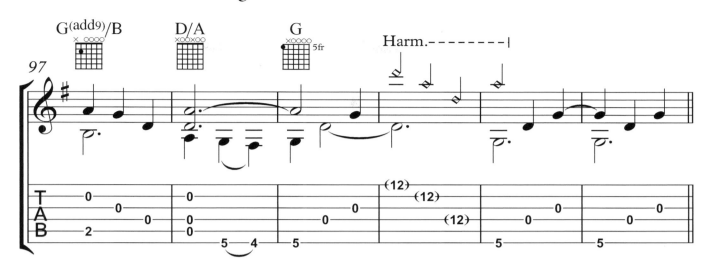

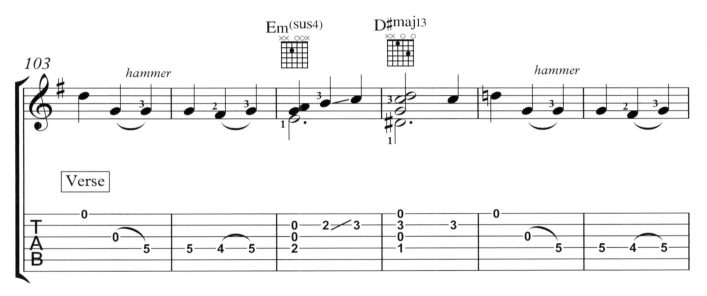

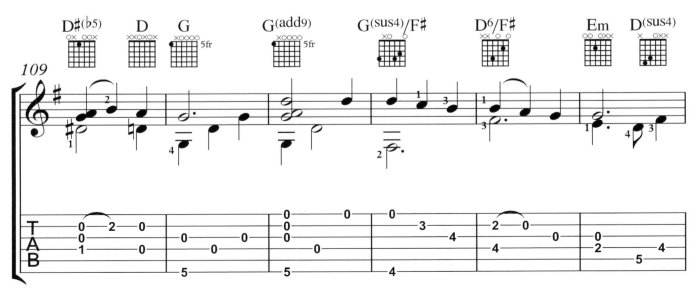

Bring a Torch, Jeanette, Isabella

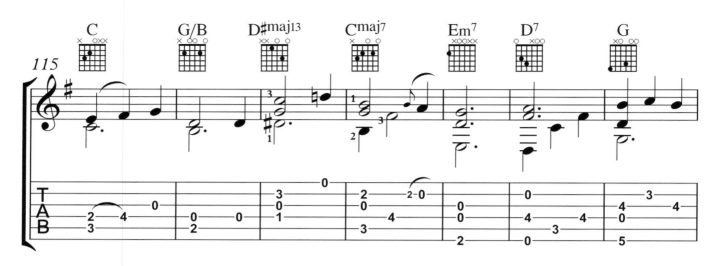

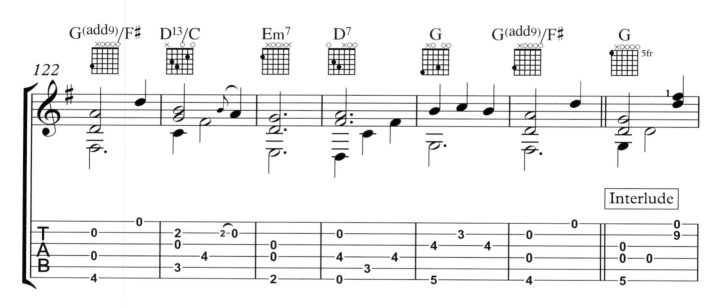

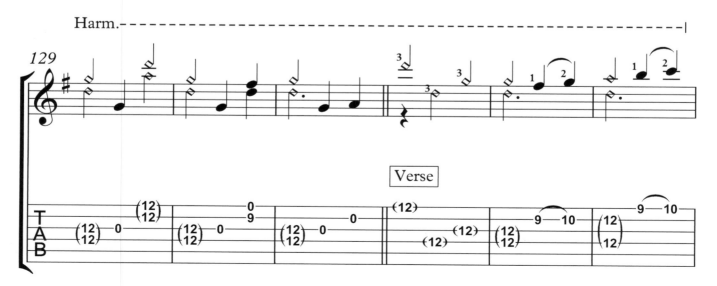

Bring a Torch, Jeanette, Isabella

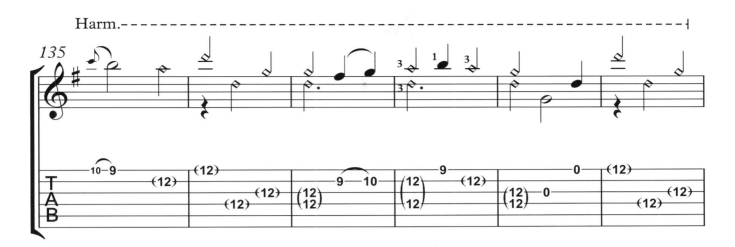

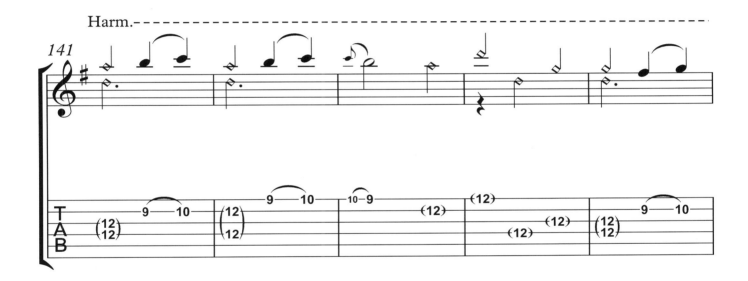

The First Noel

The First Noel is a traditional English carol dating from at least the 18th century, and perhaps as far back as the 13th century. You may also find the title spelled as *The First Nowell*. "Noel" comes from the French word for Christmas, so the song is simply about the first Christmas. Like many hymns, the melody is probably from an earlier tune. The first known publication was in William Sandy's *Christmas Carols, Ancient and Modern*, published in 1833.

The First Noel has been recorded by the Supremes, Elvis Presley, and even Bob Dylan.

This arrangement is in the key of D major, and makes frequent use of cross-string "harp" techniques. Try to keep the strings ringing as long as possible during these sections, and try for smooth transitions between chords.

There are a few tricky parts in this arrangement, especially in the second verse, starting at measure 33. Pay close attention to the fingerings in the standard notation. Also see the extended performance notes following the transcription on page 58 for some more detailed discussion and suggested alternate fingerings.

The First Noel

DADGAD Tuning

Traditional, arr. Doug Young

The First Noel

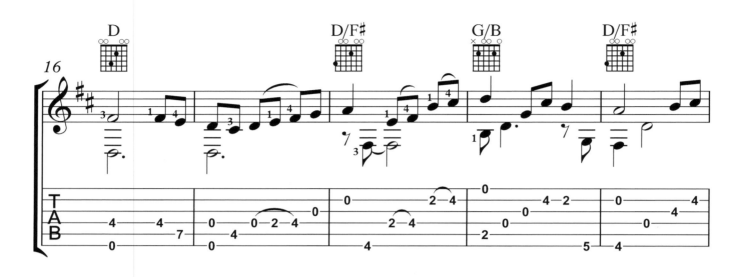

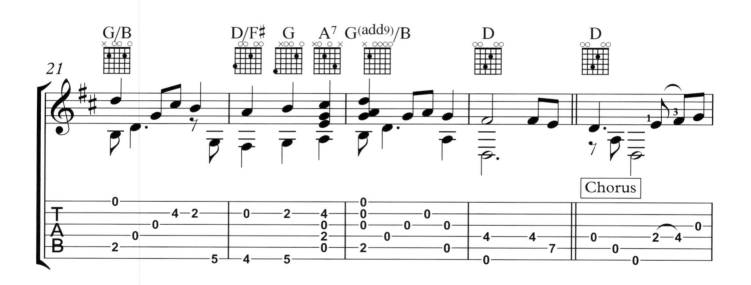

Chorus

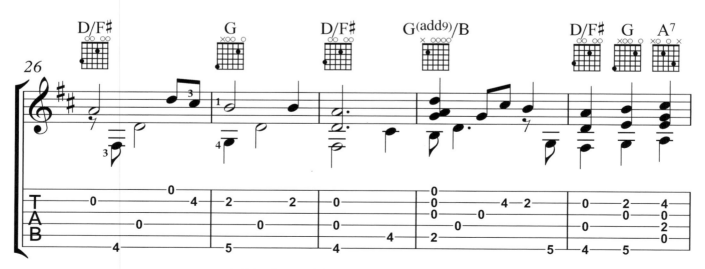

The First Noel

The First Noel

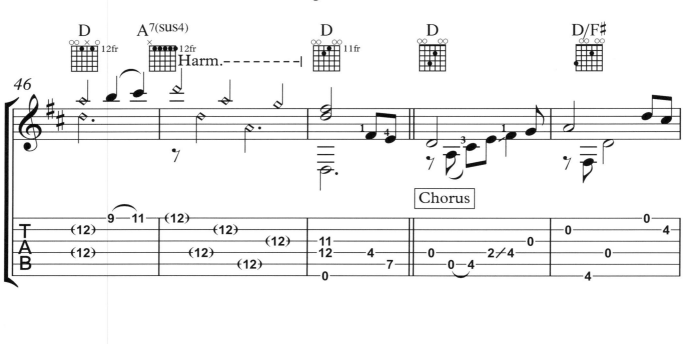

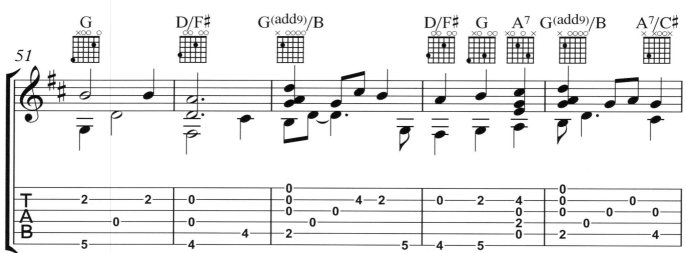

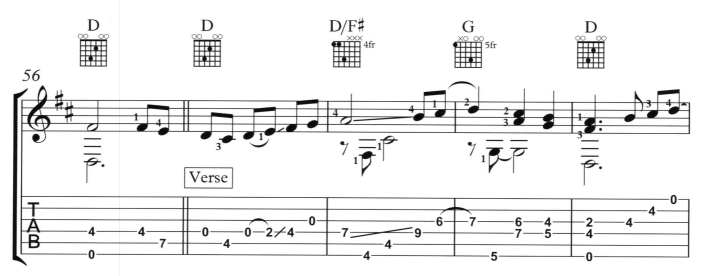

The First Noel

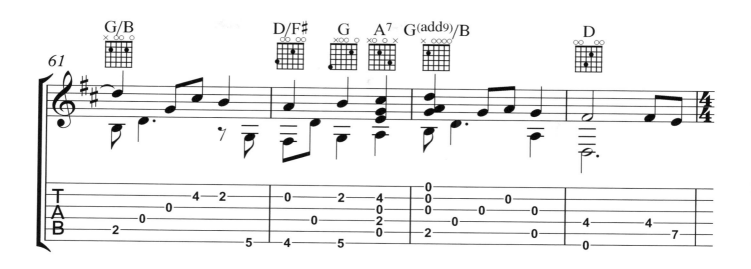

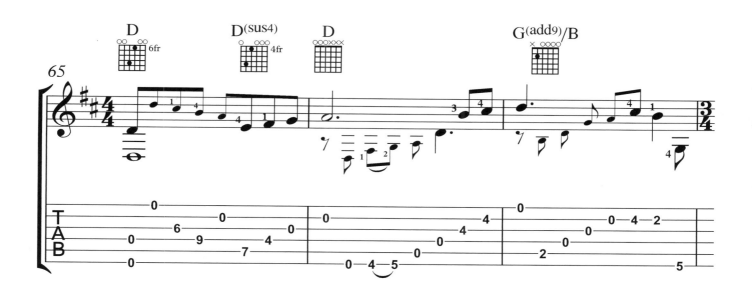

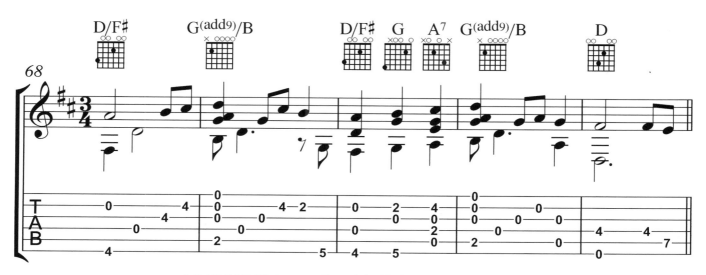

The First Noel

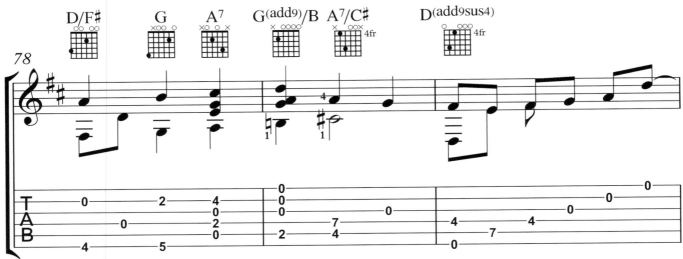

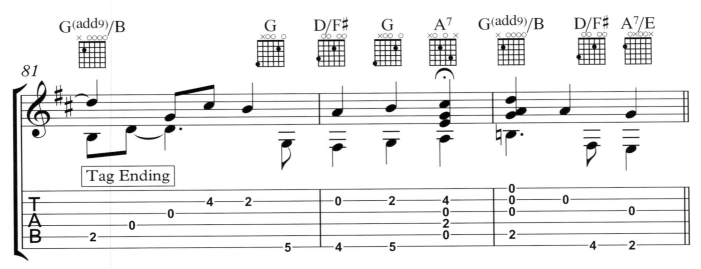

The First Noel

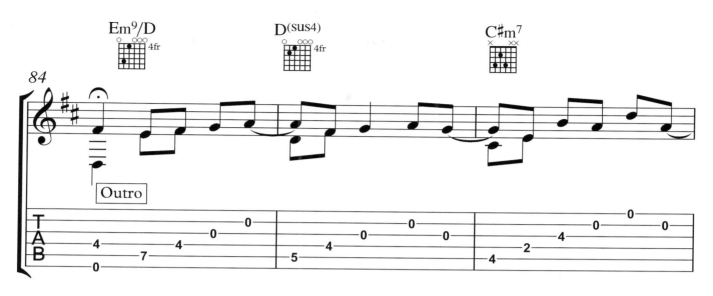

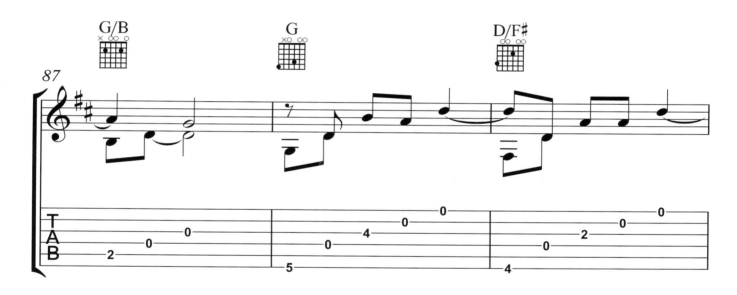

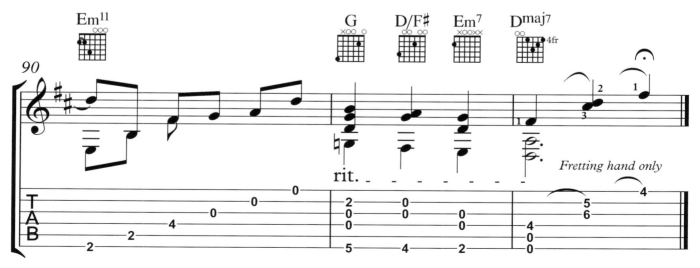

The First Noel

Alternate Fingerings

I made a few choices of fingerings in this arrangement that worked for me, but might be a bit of a stretch for some people, such as the G chord with the B on the 2nd string. I use that chord shape in several places, like this passage starting in measure 13.

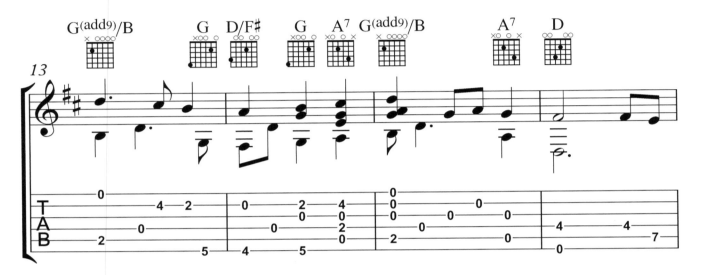

If you have trouble with the stretch, you might try fingering the chord with the B of the 3rd string, as shown below. I changed the timing a bit here. I liked the delayed G bass note in the original, but it doesn't feel right with the changed fingering, so I've changed the bass and melody to coincide, which is more conventional anyway.

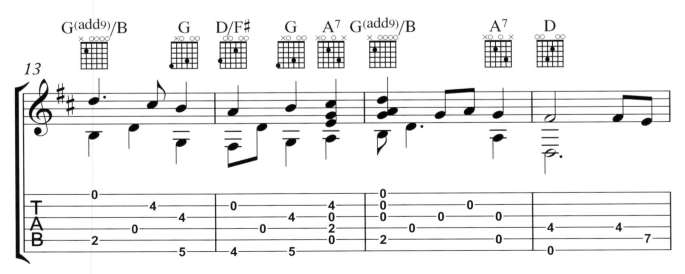

Here's yet another option for this passage, keeping much of the chord movement on the 6th and 3rd strings. The bass line and melody are harmonized 10ths.

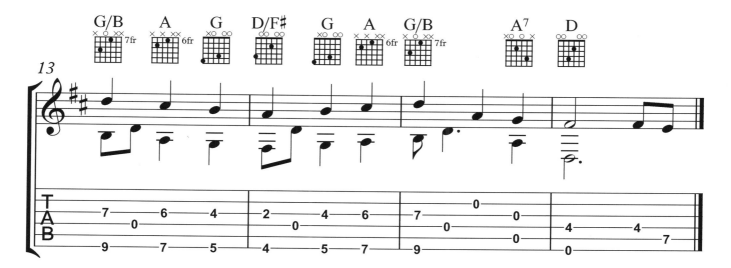

You can experiment with these alternate fingerings throughout the piece. I chose the fingerings I used to try to create smooth transitions, but with practice, any of these could work, and you might prefer another way, or might mix them up. I tend to play the tune differently each time I perform it.

Perhaps the trickiest section of this arrangement is the second verse, where the melody is played up an octave. It's difficult to maintain solid bass notes while playing near the 12th fret, so instead, I've opted for an arpeggiated approach that weaves the melody between accompaniment and harmonics in a slightly more abstract way. You may find measures 34 and 35 easier if you don't try to grab the entire chord at once. You can play the initial melody and bass notes and place your other fingers "just in time." The most important thing is to keep the melody going, so you can always drop some of the other notes to simplify things, as long as the melody is preserved.

Although these suggestions apply specifically to *The First Noel*, similar ideas can be applied to any arrangement in this book. If you find a particular chord or passage too difficult, experiment with alternatives. There are almost always multiple ways to play any section.

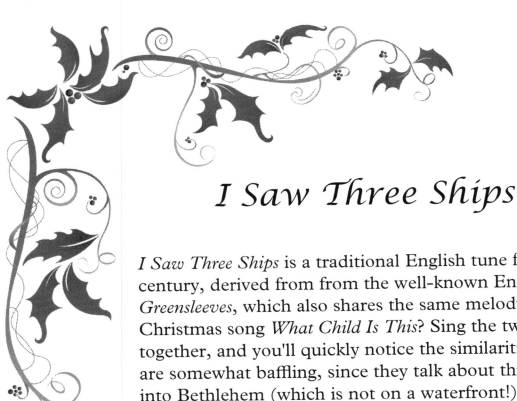

I Saw Three Ships

I Saw Three Ships is a traditional English tune from the 17th century, derived from from the well-known English tune, *Greensleeves*, which also shares the same melody as the Christmas song *What Child Is This?* Sing the two melodies together, and you'll quickly notice the similarities. The lyrics are somewhat baffling, since they talk about three ships sailing into Bethlehem (which is not on a waterfront!).

Guitarists may recognize this tune from an arrangement by John Renbourn, but the tune has also been recorded by Nat King Cole, Dan Fogelberg, Sting, and many others.

Like most treatments, my arrangement has a bit of a bounce, with a Celtic-flavored jig character. Borrowing the same technique I used with *Joy To The World*, I decided to start the arrangement with a slower, minor version of the melody. I tried to imagine that perhaps the ships are slowly arriving in an early morning fog. Then, at measure 10, we break into the major key and a jig feel.

Many guitarists have heard that DADGAD can only be used to play in the key of D. This arrangement proves otherwise, as we start in D minor, move to D major, modulate to G major, then again to C major, before returning to D. Modulating is a useful way to keep a simple repetitive tune like this interesting.

I Saw Three Ships should be straight-forward to play. Watch for the "hammer-ons-from-nowhere", in measure 10 and elsewhere. I also use various "ornaments" — pulloffs and hammers that add some variety to the melody somewhat at random throughout the tune.

I Saw Three Ships

DADGAD Tuning

Traditional, arr. Doug Young

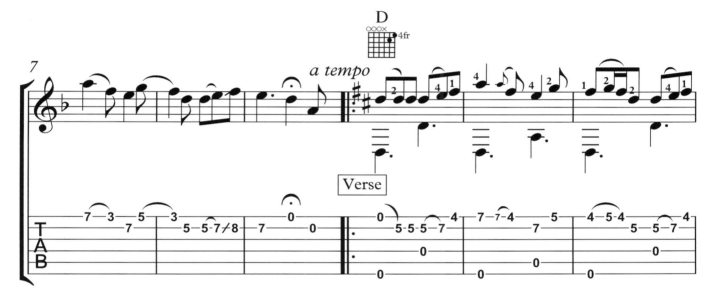

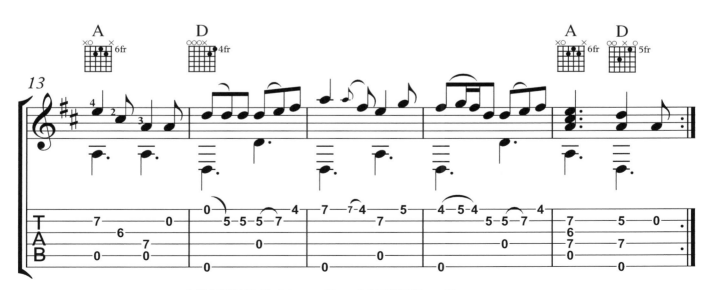

I Saw Three Ships

I Saw Three Ships

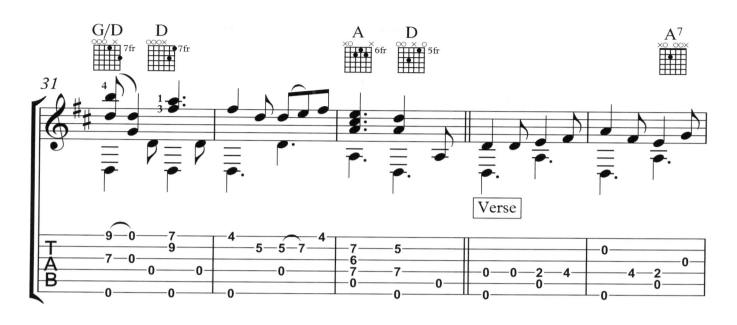

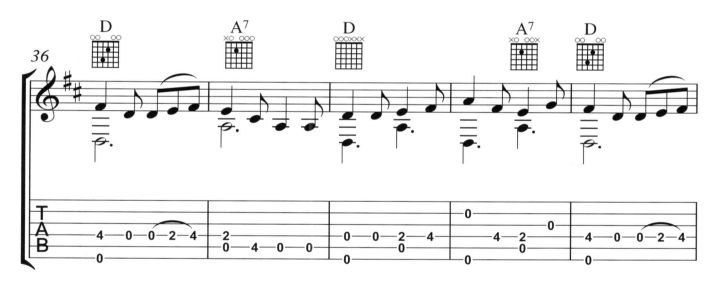

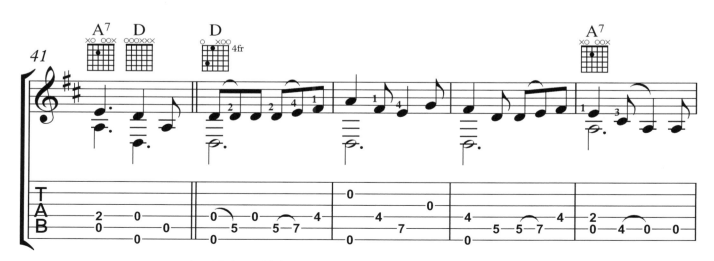

I Saw Three Ships

I Saw Three Ships

I Saw Three Ships

I Saw Three Ships

I Saw Three Ships

I Saw Three Ships

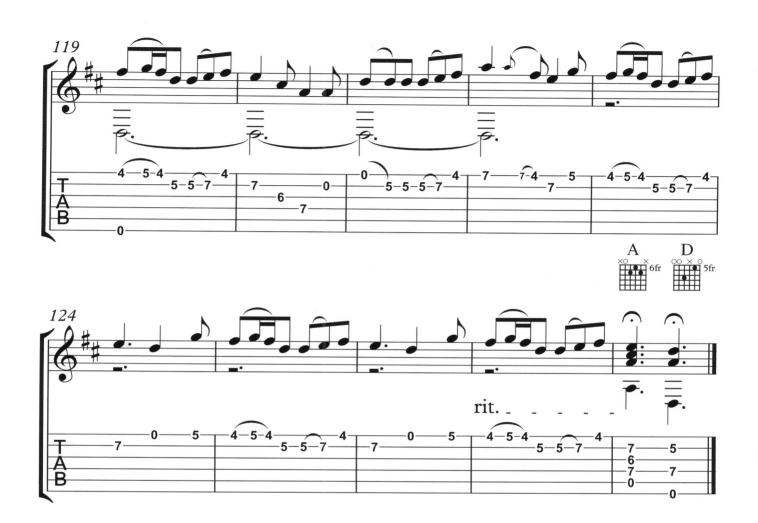

Joy To The World

Joy To The World is a triumphant anthem proclaiming the joy of the Christmas message. The lyrics were written by Isaac Watts, who published the song in 1719, in a collection titled *The Psalms of David: Imitated in the Language of the New Testament and applied to the Christian State and Worship.* Watts was clearly someone who enjoyed words! The melody was added in 1839 by Lowell Mason, based on themes by Handel.

This arrangement begins with a re-harmonized variation of the main theme, which (between a slightly slower speed and some minor chord voicings), creates a somewhat somber mood. The mood is then dramatically broken at measure 6 as we break into the familiar bright major sound of the song. I like the way this intro teases the listener, hinting at the melody in a way that is unexpected, but if you find it to be too far out, or if the fingerings are a bit of a stretch, you can always start the tune at measure 6.

Most of the arrangement is fairly straight-forward, exploring several different ways to harmonize the melody in different octaves over the predominantly D major tonality. The last verse has some more complex chords that may be a challenge to play at speed, so try not to rush the first verses. You can always slow the tune down, and it is also possible to simplify any parts you find difficult. One strategy would be to use portions of one of the earlier verses, while another would be to drop portions of some of the more challenging chord shapes.

Joy To The World

DADGAD Tuning

Watts, arr Doug Young

Joy To The World

Joy To The World

Joy To The World

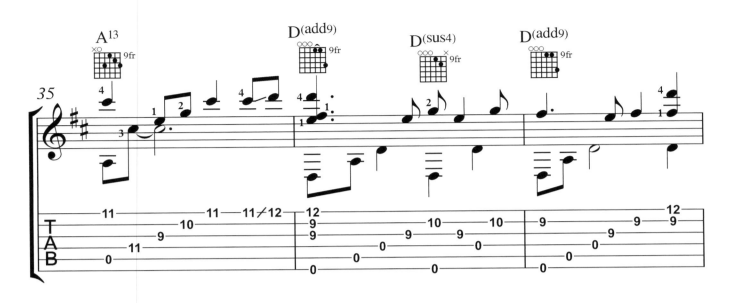

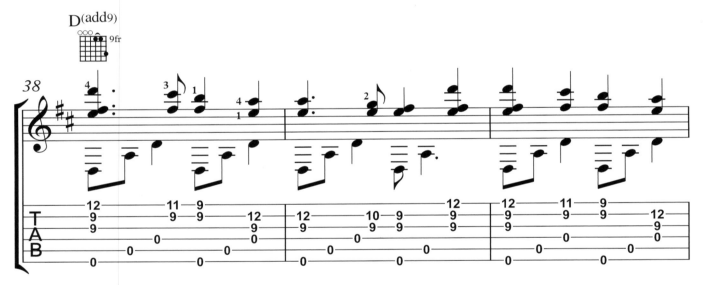

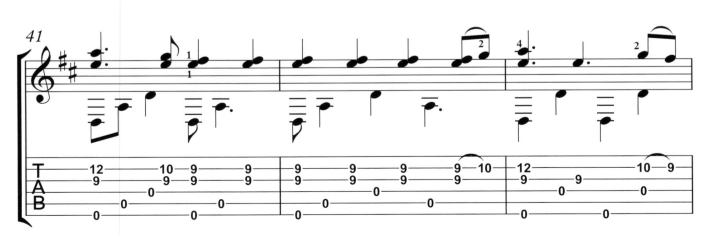

Joy To The World

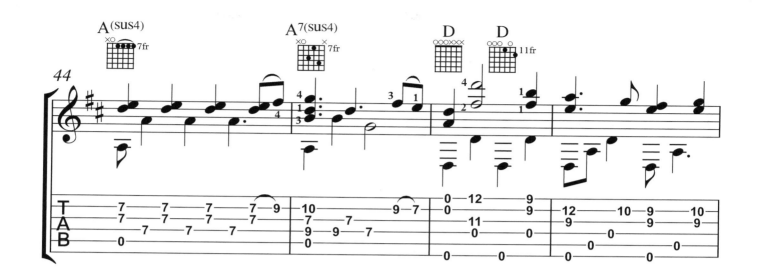

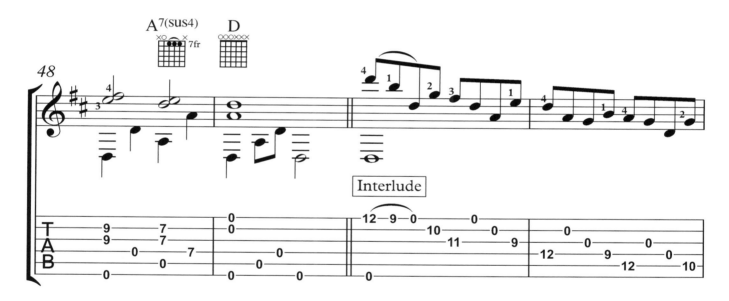

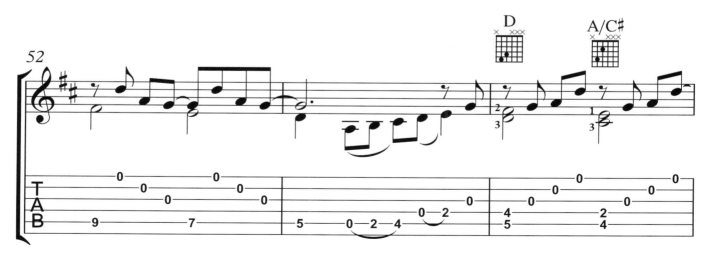

Joy To The World

Joy To The World

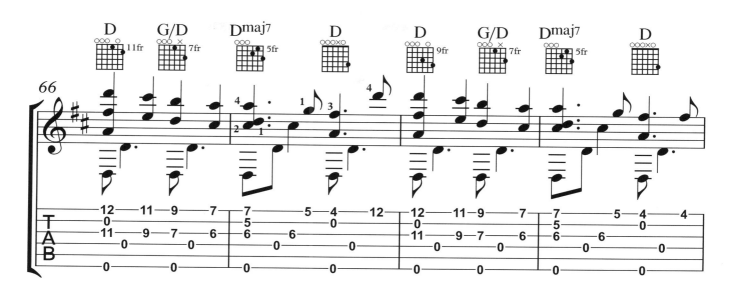

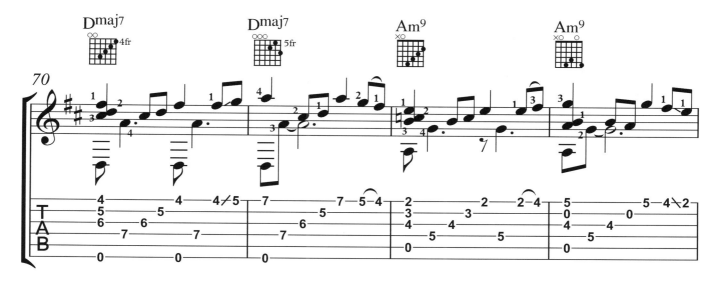

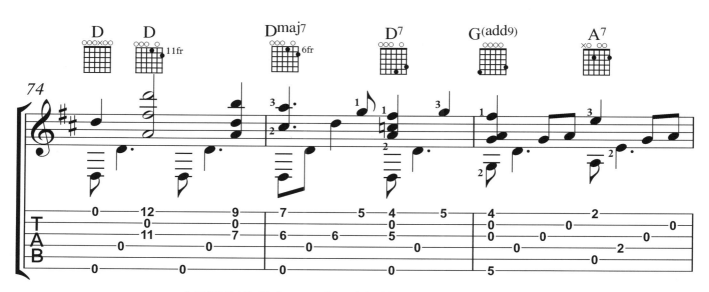

Joy To The World

O Holy Night

O Holy Night was composed in 1847 by the French operatic composer Adolphe Adam, adding music to a poem, *Minuit, Crétiens,* written earlier by a French poet, Placide Cappeau.

O Holy Night has the distinction of being the second piece of music to be broadcast on radio (in 1906). The earliest commercial recording of the tune was by Enrico Caruso. With its dramatic soaring melody, the tune has been a popular choice for modern performers like Celine Dion, Andrea Bocelli, and others.

Because *O Holy Night* is relatively long and harmonically complex, the arrangement itself can be rather straightforward. I've begun with a simple arpeggiated introduction that sets up the 6/8 feel of the tune, and then play the melody, trying to maintain a 6/8 accompaniment underneath. The tune can be repeated as many times as desired. I haven't created any specific variations, but with a tune that already has this much variety and harmonic interest, you can leverage dynamics, tempo, and phrasing to introduce your own variations.

Watch the fingerings for suggestions on how to handle some of the chord transitions. For example, in measure 30 and 31, I move to the barred F#m on the last note of measure 30. In measure 47, I switch fingers on the F# in the second half of the measure to make it easier to transition to the Em barre in measure 48. You may find other ways to make these changes smoothly, just try to avoid disrupting the flow of the accompaniment.

O Holy Night

DADGAD Tuning

Adam/Cappeau, arr Doug Young

O Holy Night

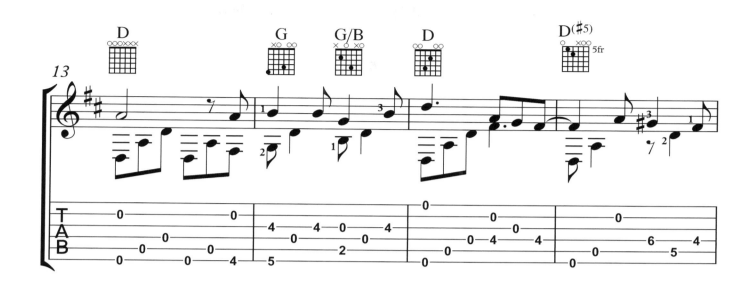

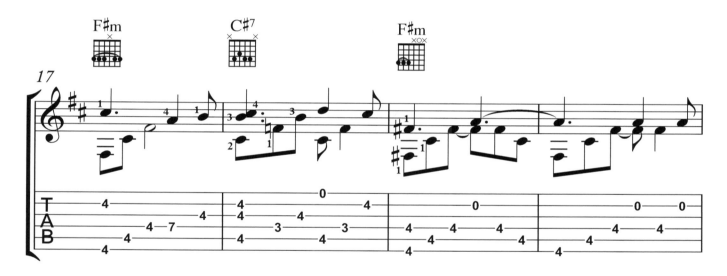

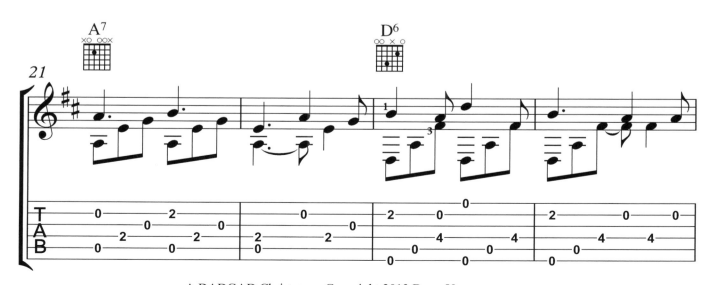

O Holy Night

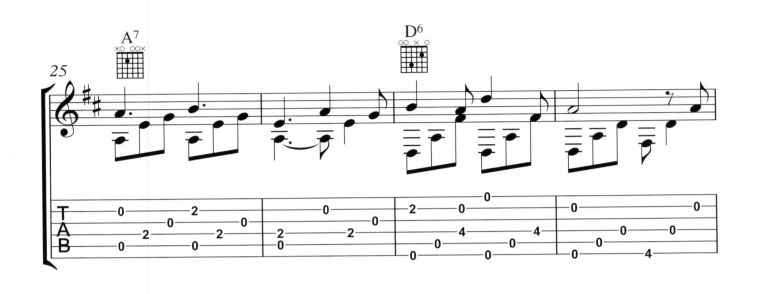

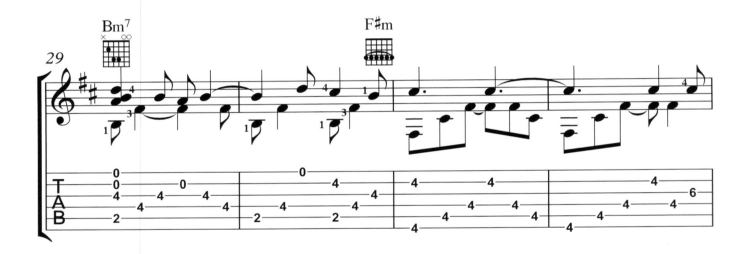

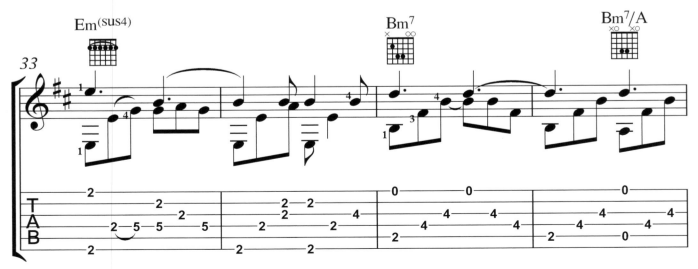

O Holy Night

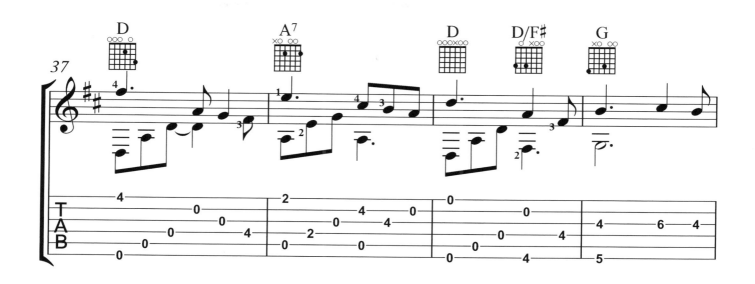

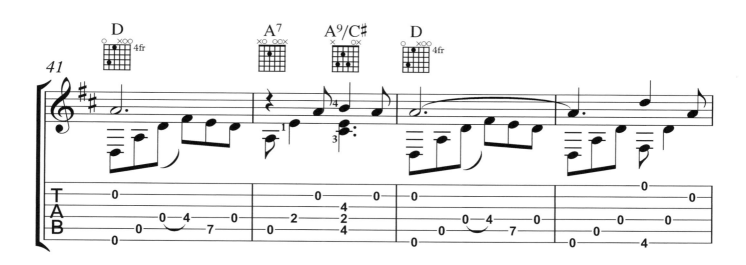

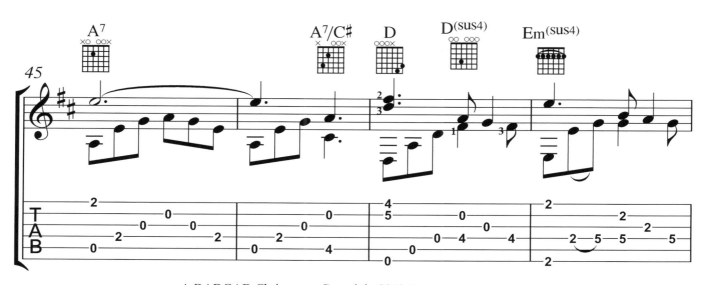

O Holy Night

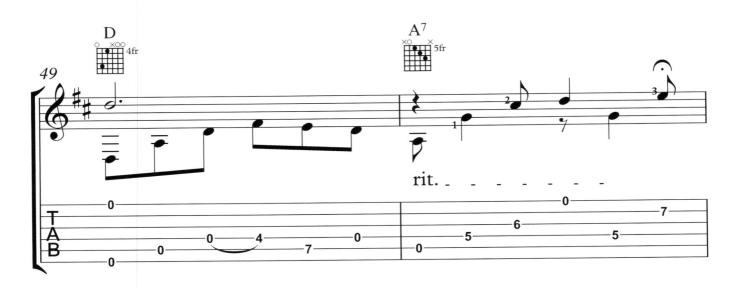

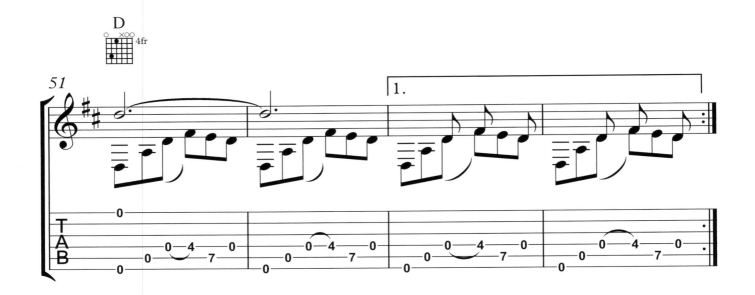

Silent Night

Silent Night is possibly the best known and most popular of all Christmas tunes. The German carol, *Stille Nacht,* was composed by school teacher and organist Franz Xaver Gruber, adding a melody to lyrics by Father Joseph Mohr. Gruber composed the tune and created guitar accompaniment, and the two co-authors gave the first performance of the piece for mass in 1818. Gruber's original tune was thought to have been fairly upbeat, but today, the beautiful melody is almost always played slowly.

For this arrangement, I've added a bell-like introduction using 12th and 7th fret harmonics, which are also used between verses. The arrangement should be easy to play, just try to bring the melody out as much as possible, especially since the accompaniment sometimes crosses the melody to a higher register.

You will also find a more basic version of *Silent Night* in the Gig Book section of this book, which explores the tune in both the key of D and the key of A.

Silent Night

DADGAD Tuning

Gruber/Mohr (1818), arr Doug Young

Silent Night

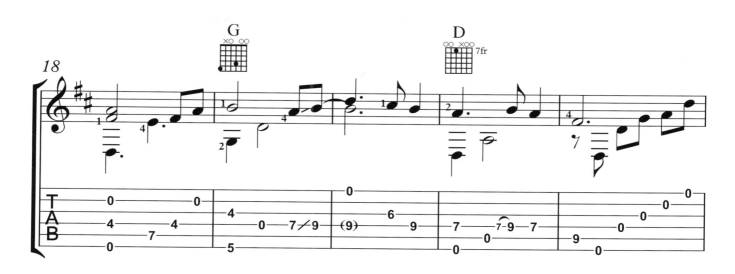

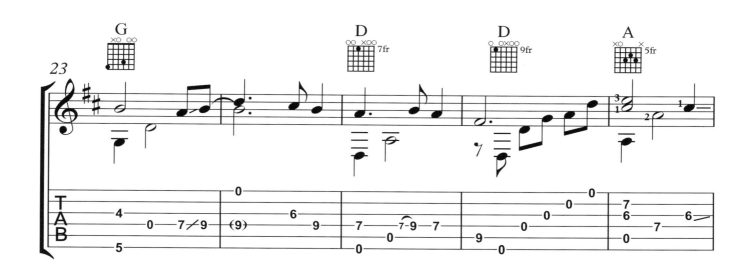

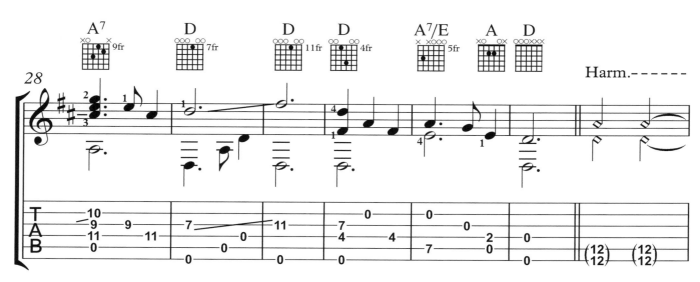

Silent Night

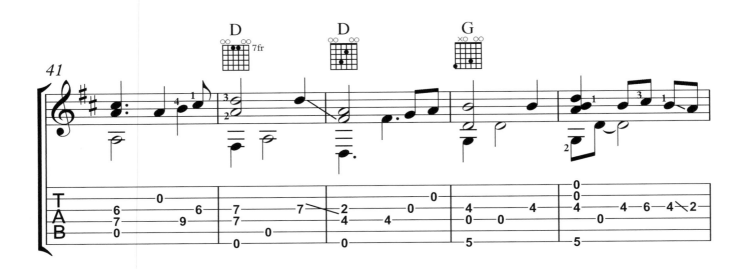

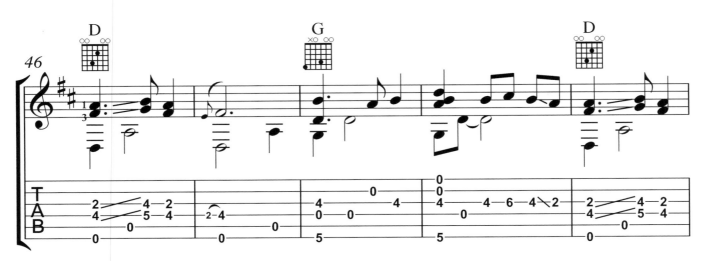

Silent Night

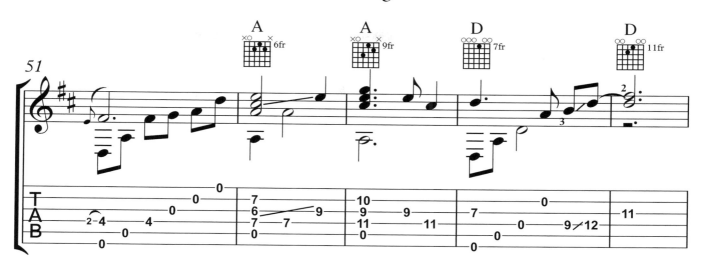

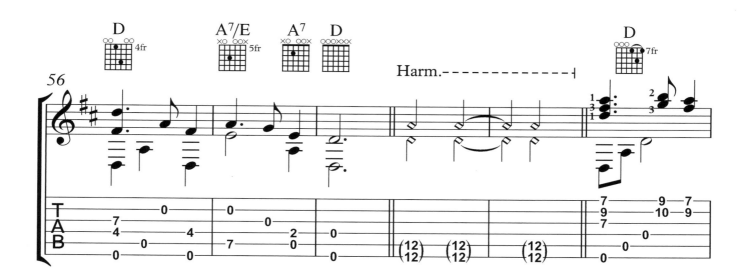

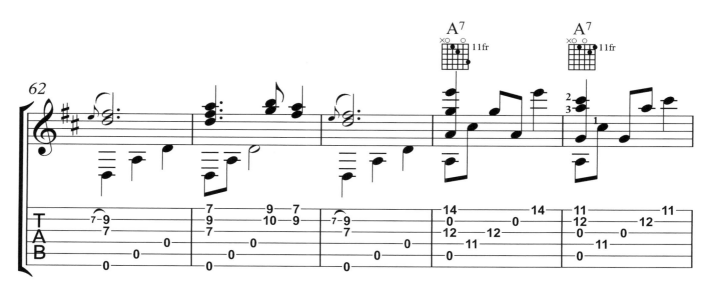

Silent Night

Silent Night

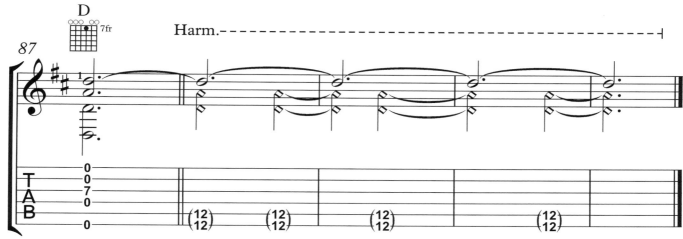

We Three Kings

We Three Kings was written by John Henry Hopkins Jr., an Episcopal deacon, in the mid 1800's. Unlike many carols that were originally written as poems and then put to music, Hopkins wrote both the music and the lyrics. The lyrics are written from the viewpoint of the Magi, the three wise men who journeyed to see Jesus at his birth.

This arrangement tries to create a bit of mystery, in keeping with the dark timbre of the minor tune. DADGAD allows us to create tight note clusters that are somewhat more difficult to achieve in standard tuning, and I'm leveraging some of those in this arrangement to produce the closely voiced chords in the introduction, as well as some even more dissonant voicings later on. This arrangement makes frequent use of open strings as drones - which hopefully helps create an exotic sound in keeping with the "*Of Orient Are*" theme. Just try to be sure to keep track of which notes are providing the melody and don't get lost among all the open ringing strings.

We Three Kings

DADGAD Tuning

Hopkins (1857), arr by Doug Young

We Three Kings

We Three Kings

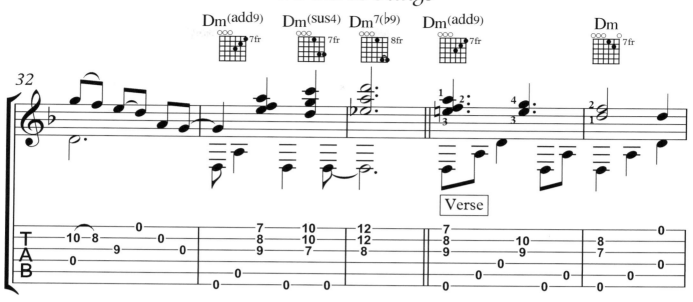

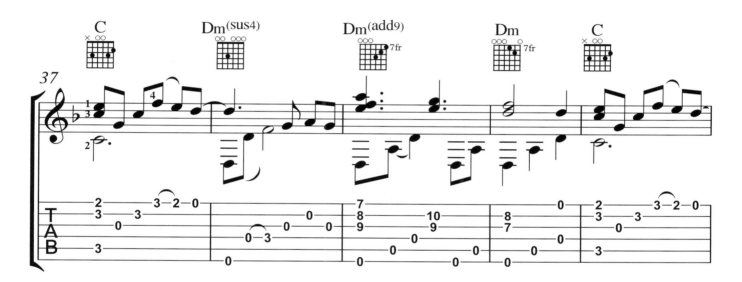

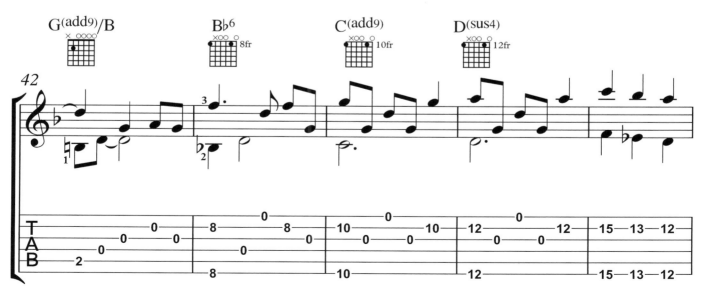

We Three Kings

We Three Kings

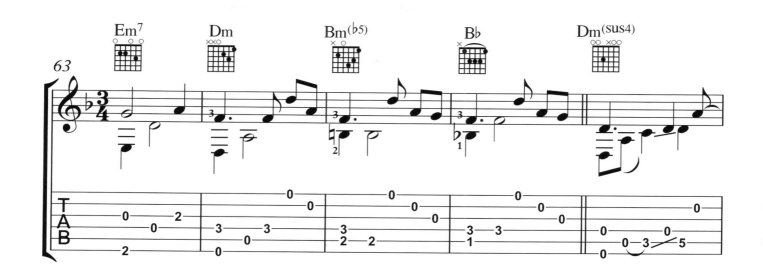

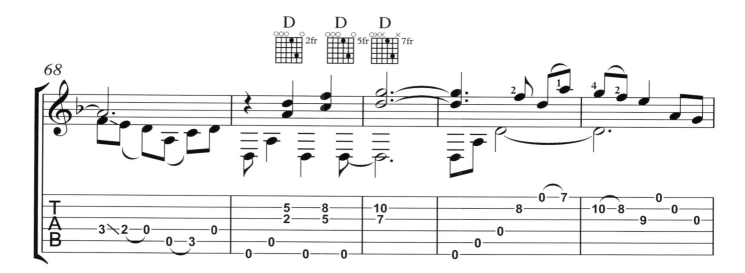

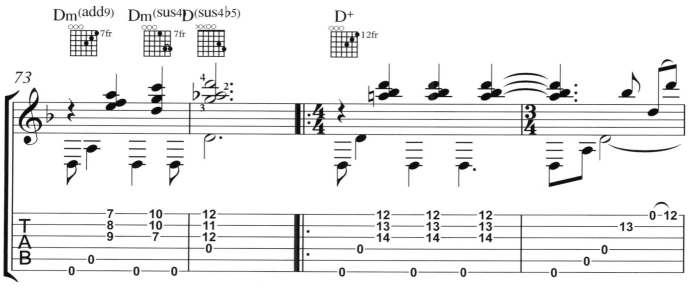

We Three Kings

We Three Kings

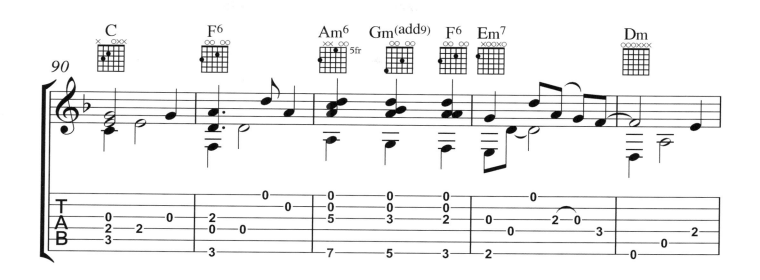

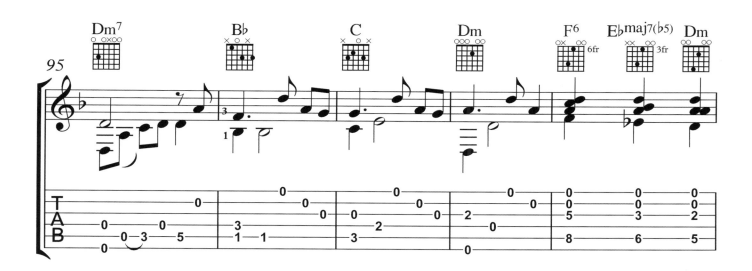

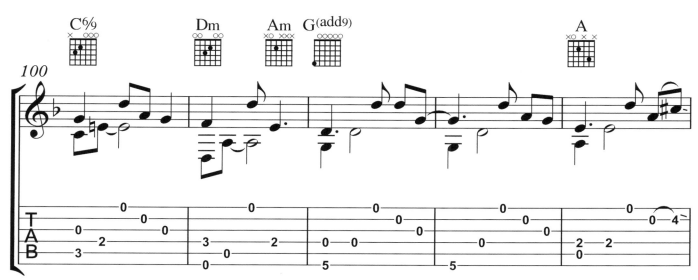

We Three Kings

We Three Kings

O Little Town of Bethlehem

O Little Town of Bethlehem was written as a poem by Phillip Brooks in 1868, following a trip to Bethlehem. The poem was put to music by Lewis Redner.

My arrangement of this tune came to me at the last minute, while putting the final touches on this book, and it seemed like a fitting ending. It's short – I've only arranged it as a single verse. I'm thinking of it as a simple, sweet "bookend," that might be appropriate to close out a set or a CD.

There are some fairly complex chords in the arrangement, and I'm playing it slowly and very rubato, to bring out the color notes in each chord. The arrangement also uses a few tricky fingerings, so pay close attention to the chord shapes and the fingerings indicated in the standard notation. There are ways to simplify many of the chords, and as with any of these arrangements, you may prefer alternate fingerings in some places.

O Little Town of Bethlehem

DADGAD Tuning

Brooks/Redner (circa 1868), arr Doug Young

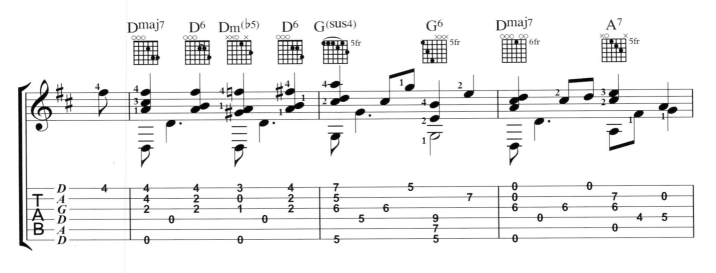

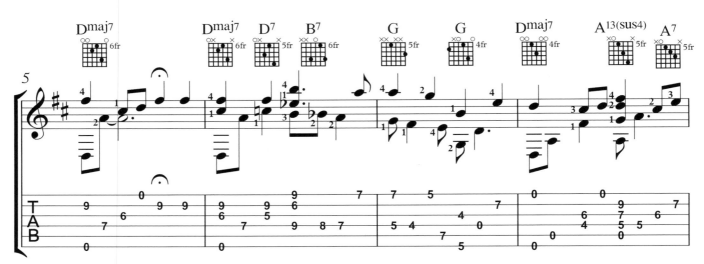

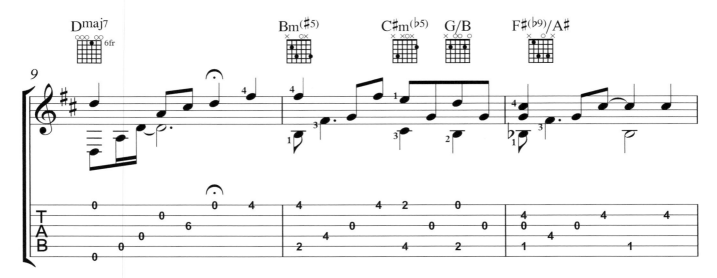

O Little Town of Bethlehem

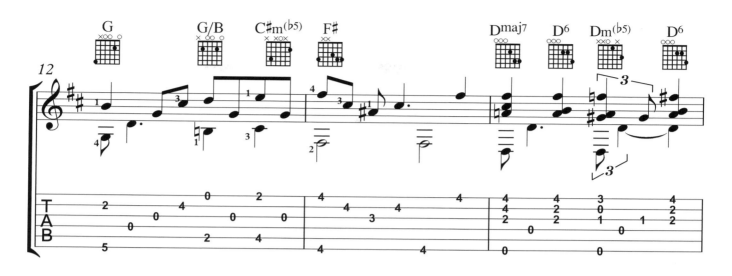

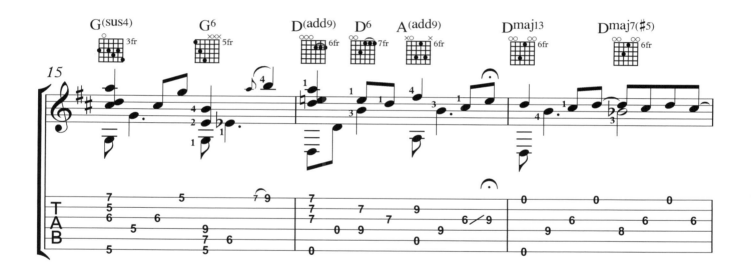

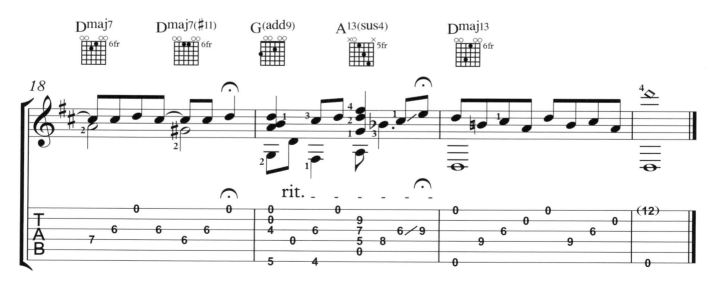

Merry Christmas!

Doug Young

Manufactured by Amazon.ca
Bolton, ON

34818736R00061